Hindmarch

With the collaboration of

Larry L. Cummings   University of Wisconsin

Martin G. Evans   University of Toronto

W. Clay Hamner   Duke University

Edward E. Lawler, III   University of Michigan

Edwin A. Locke   University of Maryland

Fred Luthans   University of Nebraska

William E. Scott, Jr.   Indiana University

Patricia Cain Smith   Bowling Green State University

Steven Kerr, *Discussant*   University of Southern California

POINT & COUNTERPOINT

IN ORGANIZATIONAL BEHAVIOR

BARBARA KARMEL

Atkinson Graduate School of Administration
Willamette University

THE DRYDEN PRESS

HINSDALE, ILLINOIS

© 1980 by The Dryden Press
A division of Holt, Rinehart and Winston, Publishers

Library of Congress Catalog Card Number: 78-65380

ISBN: 0-03-054686-9

Printed in the United States of America

Press of W. B. Saunders Company

Last digit is the print number: 9   8   7   6   5   4   3   2   1

CHARLOTTE REED MARBUT
1895 - 1978

In Memoriam

PREFACE

The book you are about to read was born in the summer of 1977 at the Academy of Management Annual Meeting in Orlando, Florida. Assembled there was an audience of 300 or so people, four pairs of debaters, a discussant, a cardholder, and a chairman of the session. The title of the symposium was "Point and Counterpoint in Organizational Behavior." The rules of debate were that each debater was allowed four minutes to make an initial presentation, three minutes to rebut his or her opponent, and one minute to summarize. That is why this is a relatively short book.

The debates were, with the permission of the debaters, tape-recorded. Soon after the session, the chairman began to receive requests for transcriptions of the symposium. The debaters, understandably, were given an opportunity to edit their remarks. (It isn't easy to be cool and articulate when 300 people are watching, one's distinguished colleague is attacking, and only eight minutes are allowed.) Before long it was clear that many people who were not at the session and some who were had a great deal of interest in reading the edited comments of the debaters and discussant. This interest is in part attributable to the topic areas and content of the debates and in part to the eminence of the speakers. Biographical sketches included at the beginning of each chapter will give you a sense of the accomplishments of the participants, but in the interest of brevity they fall far short of a comprehensive picture of the contributions each has made to the discipline of organizational behavior. The consolidated resumés of these scholars might be longer than the book itself. While these speakers are very different as personalities, in physical appearance, and in their perspectives on the discipline, they have in common outstanding skills of presentation and knowledge of the field. As chairman of the symposium and now editor of this volume, I am sincerely grateful to them for undertaking a difficult task. To their great credit, they have honored my request to present the advantages of one, and only one, view of human behavior and to avoid compromise positions that would have seemed more reasonable but been less effective in demonstrating differences of opinion during the debate.

Where did the original idea for this symposium come from? Like most good ideas it came from a coincidence of several events. My son, who is a high school debater, observed at the conclusion of a Shana Alexander and James Kilpatrick debate on "60 Minutes" on arms shipment to the Middle East that time for rebuttal would certainly enhance the viewers' understanding of the issues. I observed that the debate format, with or without rebuttal, helped me understand the underlying issues much better than a descriptive, editorial examination would have. Some days later I was present at the 4th Biennial Leadership Conference at Southern Illinois University and heard an informal debate — some would say an argument — between Bill Scott and Bob House on the subject of leadership. Why not, I thought, find a way to provide this kind of learning experience for a larger audience, with a wider representation of speakers and topics? A symposium was born. The proposal for a symposium was reviewed by the Organizational Behavior Division of the Academy of Management and was, as noted, presented at the Annual Meeting. The audience, principally professors of organizational behavior, responded enthusiastically to this unusual event. At the very least it was more lively than the usual reading of research papers.

The next step, and in many ways the most difficult, was finding a publisher who would publish the transcriptions as a book. It took time and perseverance, until January of 1978, to accomplish this feat. My thanks, and I hope yours, go the the patient people at W. B. Saunders Company, principally Jack Neifert and Wayne Koch, who undertook this job as a "service to the profession" (that means in expectation of a valuable contribution at no profit). In the following months, the debaters completed the editing of their remarks, still observing my admonition to retain the basic content and theme of the original debates. Steve Kerr did likewise, although I do not remember his excellent street lamp metaphor in the original version. Finally, I have supplied introductory and summary material written during my transition from the University of Wisconsin in Madison to Willamette University in Salem, Oregon. It has not been an easy task; books never are, but the introductory material in this particular book carries the heavy burden of providing a sense of perspective and a structure on which the reader can hang a complex array of ideas.

There are, along the way, some aides to the reader, student or instructor. Following this preface is a matrix detailing the "fit" between these chapters and the content of a number of textbooks on organizational behavior. It is strongly suggested that the appropriate chapter of the textbook be read *before* embarking on each debate. In Chapter 2 there are suggestions for interpreting and using the debate format as a classroom exercise. I have found this most productive and stimulating in my own classroom. For those who are hungry for more information on the various topics, each debater has supplied a list of references and recommended readings at the end of each chapter. At the end of the book, there is a glossary of words and phrases. The definitions were not easy to secure unanimity for, and therefore occasionally two definitions are given that reflect differences in usage of the phrase, or disagreement as to its meaning, or both.

A final word of thanks to the cardholder, my friend and colleague Professor Patrick Connor of Oregon State University, who agreed in a weak moment to be the "timer" for these debates. He held cards reading four, three, two, one, one-half and 0 minutes left up to the speaker. Because his total attention was given to watching his timepiece instead of listening to the debates, he will receive a free copy of this book. Every debater stopped talking on time—no mean feat for nine college professors.

BARBARA KARMEL
Salem, Oregon

KEY TO TEXTBOOK IN ORGANIZATIONAL BEHAVIOR

Authors	Albanese	Behling and Schreisheim	Coffey et al.	Dressler	Filley and House
Title	Management: Toward Accounting for Performance	Organizational Behavior: Theory, Research and Application	Behavior in Organizations: A Multidimensional View	Organizations and Management	Managerial Processes and Organizational Behavior
Publisher	Irwin	Allyn-Bacon	Prentice-Hall	Prentice-Hall	Scott-Foresman
Year	1978	1976	1975	1976	1969

Chapter numbers shown in the matrix below are keyed to the topic areas of each debate. Where possible, it is desirable to assign chapters keyed for both motivation and organizational behavior modification before assigning these two debates.

POINT AND COUNTERPOINT	Chapter	Chapter	Chapter	Chapter	Chapter
3. Motivation	6	4	9	9	15
4. Organizational Behavior Modification	8	3 and 10	8	9	17
5. Task Design	16	11	12	4	9
6. Leadership*	11	12	8	7	16

* Since this debate summarizes preceding material, all referenced chapters should have been read by students before they embark on Chapter 6 of *Point and Counterpoint.*

Authors	Haiman, Scott and Connor	Hamner and Organ	Hellriegel and Slocum	Herbert	Hodgetts and Altman
Title	Managing the Modern Organization	Applied Behavior: An Applied Psychological Approach	Organizational Behavior Contingency Views	Dimensions of Organizational Behavior	Organizational Behavior
Publisher	Houghton-Mifflin	Business Publications, Inc.	West	Macmillan	W. B. Saunders
Year	1978	1978	1976	1976	1979

POINT AND COUNTERPOINT	Chapter	Chapter	Chapter	Chapter	Chapter
3. Motivation	24	7	9	11 and 12	5
4. Organizational Behavior Modification	24	11	4	21	4
5. Task Design	24	12	9	22	12
6. Leadership*	24	17	10	18	9

* Since this debate summarizes preceding material, all referenced chapters should have been read by students before they embark on Chapter 6 of *Point and Counterpoint.*

KEY TO TEXTBOOKS IN ORGANIZATIONAL BEHAVIOR (Con't)

Authors	Huse and Bowditch	Ivancevich, Szilagi and Wallace	Luthans	Porter et al.
Title	Behavior in Organizations: A Systems Approach	Organizational Behavior and Performance	Organizational Behavior	Behavior in Organizations
Publisher	Addison-Wesley	Goodyear	McGraw-Hill	McGraw-Hill
Year	1977	1977	1977	1975

POINT AND COUNTERPOINT	Chapter	Chapter	Chapter	Chapter
3. Motivation	3	3 and 5	13 and 17	2
4. Organizational Behavior Modification	3	4	12	7
5. Task Design	12	6	19	10
6. Leadership*	7	10	18	14

* Since this debate summarizes preceding material, all referenced chapters should have been read by students before they embark on Chapter 6 of *Point and Counterpoint.*

Authors	Reitz	Sayles and Strauss	Tosi and Hamner	
Title	Behavior in Organizations	Human Behavior in Organizations	Organizational Behavior and Management: A Contingency Approach	
Publisher	Irwin	Prentice-Hall	St. Clair	
Year	1977	1976	1974	

POINT AND COUNTERPOINT	Chapter	Chapter	Chapter	
3. Motivation	3 and 4	6	Part III-C	
4. Organizational Behavior Modification	5	6	V	
5. Task Design	5	3	VII	
6. Leadership*	20	9	VI	

* Since this debate summarizes preceding material, all referenced chapters should have been read by students before they embark on Chapter 6 of *Point and Counterpoint.*

CONTENTS

Part I

INTRODUCTION 1

Chapter 1.

ISSUES AND THEMES IN ORGANIZATIONAL BEHAVIOR 3

Barbara Karmel, Willamette University

Chapter 2.

WHY DEBATES? 11

Barbara Karmel, Willamette University

Part II

THE DEBATES 15

Chapter 3.

MOTIVATION 17

Edwin A. Locke, University of Maryland
W. Clay Hamner, Duke University

Chapter 4.

ORGANIZATIONAL BEHAVIOR MODIFICATION 47

Fred Luthans, University of Nebraska
Patricia Cain Smith, Bowling Green University

Chapter 5.

TASK DESIGN 95

Edward E. Lawler, III, University of Michigan
Larry L. Cummings, University of Wisconsin

Chapter 6.

LEADERSHIP 109

William E. Scott, Jr., Indiana University
Martin G. Evans, University of Toronto

Part III
CONCLUSION 139

  Chapter 7.

COMMENTS BY THE DISCUSSANT 141

  Steven Kerr, University of Southern California

  Chapter 8.

SUMMARY AND RECOMMENDATIONS 147

  Barbara Karmel, Willamette University

GLOSSARY OF WORDS AND PHRASES 151

Part I

INTRODUCTION

CHAPTER 1   Issues and Themes in Organizational Behavior
CHAPTER 2   Why Debates?

BARBARA KARMEL

Barbara Karmel is Associate Dean for Research and Professor of Organizational Behavior at Willamette University's Atkinson Graduate School of Administration. She holds a Ph.D. in Organizational Psychology from Purdue University and has served on the faculties of the University of Wisconsin, Madison, and Oregon State University, Corvallis. She is a member of the American Psychological Association, past member of the Board of Governors and former Program Chairman of the OB Division of the Academy of Management, and is a member of the editorial board of the *Academy of Management Review*.

Dr. Karmel's articles have appeared in the *Academy of Management Review*, *Organizational Behavior and Human Performance*, *Journal of Educational Psychology*, *American Journal of Hospital Pharmacy* and *Contemporary Psychology*. As Director of the newly established Center for Business-Government Studies at Willamette, she oversees the conduct of research and dissemination of information to improve relationships between private and public sectors.

Chapter 1

ISSUES AND THEMES IN ORGANIZATIONAL BEHAVIOR

The discipline of organizational behavior (OB) has its roots in many branches of social science. It is an eclectic discipline borrowing primarily from psychology and sociology, with contributions from such diverse fields as economics, cultural anthropology, philosophy and, more recently, physiology. As an independent discipline (one knows it has achieved this status because doctorates are awarded in it and it has its own journals), it is a relative infant. Many of its senior scholars were trained as psychologists or sociologists and have adopted an organizational focus, that is, have identified a primary interest in *interactions* between individuals and organizations. This focus on person-environment interactions resulted in emphasis on certain topic areas, or variables, which in turn define the domain of organizational behavior. In broad general terms, these variables fall into two categories: Job satisfaction and performance of the individual, and factors that are presumed to affect satisfaction and performance, such as group membership, individual needs and job characteristics. Whether such organizational factors as structure of the organization, technology or climate properly "belong" to organizational behavior or to its sister discipline, organizational theory, depends on whom you ask. We will not debate this boundary line but rather suggest that it is permeable; neither discipline can or should ignore the variables that are primarily identified with the other. What is important is the recognition that organizational behavior is the study of people and their behavior as members of organizations. As in the study of human behavior in general, complexities abound. For instance, the organization does not stand still while we are conducting studies and investigations. We do not have direct access to the minds of human beings, psychologically speaking. In addition, behavior is influenced by both internal states and external events. Individuals have unique psychological characteristics. Scientists who study organizational behavior also have unique individual needs and perceptions, no matter how objective their intent.

With this brief introduction to the domain and difficulties inherent in the study of organizational behavior, let us turn to the purpose and plan of this book. It is a very nontraditional book which contains many disquieting and provocative ideas. The reader is likely to come away from it feeling both a sense of gratitude for clarification of complex issues and a sense of intellectual irritation, which, we hope, will offer a challenge to the mind and trigger the pursuit of synthesis and understanding on the part of student, manager or scholar. The choice of a debate format rather than the standard-dry descriptive writing is purely intentional; the rationale for this decision will be provided in Chapter 2. Chapters 3 through 6 contain debates between distinguished scientists, each of whom has special expertise in the topic area on which he or she debates. Chapter 7 provides the reader with insightful analysis by a discussant whose role is to extract common themes and elements from the four debates, in case the reader needs assistance in this task, as well as to provide suggestions for reconciling the very different points of view expressed in the debates. The discussant, Steve Kerr, makes no claim that he is providing the definitive commentary on the state of the discipline; instead, he double-dares the reader to think, and think hard, about ideas. Chapter 8 is reserved for the editor who gives a last word or two about the state of the discipline, the usefulness of debates, and some recommendations for improving the art, science and application of concepts in the discipline of organizational behavior. Finally, in the Appendix we supply a glossary of words and phrases to enlighten the novice and remind the expert that semantic precision is its own reward.

If the reader is not by now convinced to read on, the following *raison d'être* may be helpful. This book is intended to be a supplement to the traditional processes by which a discipline is learned, taught and applied. For the scientist who designs studies and interprets their results, the book will serve as a potent reminder of the hazards of personal values intruding upon science and of the importance of acknowledging underlying assumptions about the nature of man. For the advanced student, the debates themselves will provide a useful platform from which to launch an intensive discussion of ways and means to improve research strategies. If, on the other hand, the reader is enrolled in a first course in organizational behavior, the book is likely to serve a very different purpose. The "intro" student, at the end of the usually required OB course, will be likely to observe that he or she has been exposed to contradictory research findings, given no "rules" to explain behavior, and told that decisions about managing the human resource require careful consideration of the person and environment fit—a judgment call. This is largely true, but on the job one is confronted with such questions as:

Why do my co-workers reject me in my summer job?

Why do people sometimes sabotage equipment? How can it be stopped?

Why does the introduction of a computer make so many people unhappy?

Is there a way to increase satisfaction and productivity at the same time?

Why don't subordinates obey? They're being paid to do a job.

What can I do about flake-offs?

How can the study of organizational behavior in general, or reading this book in particular, help answer such questions? In the abstract, the study of organizational behavior helps one to understand the complexity and interdependence of factors which impinge upon the individual and affect attitudes and behaviors. In particular, this book provides the reader with an understandable, visible, articulated demonstration of differences of opinion between experts at a very fundamental level: their beliefs about the nature of men and motives. In some cases, these differences may ultimately be resolved by theory-testing research and integrated theoretical propositions. In the meanwhile, and for the practitioner, it is crucially important to be knowledgeable about the sources and implications of differing beliefs, the better to examine one's own assumptions about human behavior. Out of this understanding one can begin to design a program to deal with employee dissatisfaction or low productivity, to change undesirable behavior, to select among techniques involving reward, punishment, attitude change or job redesign, and to assess the probable consequences of such procedures. In short, the book will provide a basis for understanding fundamentally different assumptions about behavior and assist the reader in identifying his or her beliefs. It should then become apparent that these beliefs color perceptions of the world and decisions about personal behavior. Being able to articulate one's own philosophy and its implications is the cornerstone of a coherent management strategy for dealing with motivational problems.

As noted earlier, the discipline of organizational behavior is fraught with conceptual and methodological problems. The following section describes some of these problems as background for understanding their emergence in the debates.

CONCEPTUAL AND METHODOLOGICAL PROBLEMS IN ORGANIZATIONAL BEHAVIOR

At the head of this list must be the problem of *terminology*. For example, what is job satisfaction? You know; I know; everybody knows. Would we agree on a definition? Is it feeling good about your job, not being unhappy, feeling a sense of acceptance, acting in ways which manifest a sense of well-being (smiling) or which do not indicate rebellion (being deliberately late)? How would we know a satisfied employee if we saw one? This one variable, job satisfaction, serves as an elegant example, since it epitomizes a number of variables in organizational behavior that suffer from lack of clear definition. Climate? Leadership? Performance? Achievement need? Group cohesiveness? The list is endless. Indeed, a recent study by Pierce and

Dunham (1978) suggests that variables found in OB studies may be very similar in conceptual content to variables called by other names in the organizational theory literature. Caution, reader! In the debates, and in OB textbooks, watch out for differences in interpretation of the words that describe variables. At the very least, try to infer from context or operationalization what meaning the debator or writer attaches to these terms and beware the situation in which the two debators are using different meanings for the same word or phrase.

A second and equally important problem in this and many other scientific disciplines is the correlation-causation distinction. Because two events (or ideas) are related or associated does not necessarily mean that they are *causally* related. For example, you may observe that there is a high correlation between reading textbooks and falling asleep. Does this mean that reading causes sleep? That feeling sleepy causes you to choose reading rather than some other activity? Both? Or are both of these events explained by (caused by) some other factor? Any of these are possible. No one of these attributions is necessarily true. The error of *attributing causality*, inferring a cause and effect relationship, from correlational or associational data is a common and dangerous one. If you observe that happy workers are productive and unhappy workers are not, it is incorrect to assume that being satisfied *causes* workers to be productive. It would be equally incorrect to assume the reverse, that being productive causes people to be satisfied. Yet, in our constant search to understand the reasons for things, we often attribute causality when the observable evidence is merely correlational. The first debate, in particular, is very much concerned with the implications of this error. It is charged that one theoretical stance is more subject to the error than another.

A number of the debators discuss the role of independent (IV), mediating (MV) and dependent (DV) variables, an area related to the causality attribution problem. Reader, please note the implicit assumption that an IV→MV→DV model attributes causality because it infers directionality in the relationship between IV and DV. The debators will have a great deal to say about this.

A third problem is generic in the social sciences and is the consequence of imprecise definitions of terms or variables. It is the *measurement* problem. The measurement of a concept such as job satisfaction is a sticky business. Should it be measured by this scale or that? Do these scales measure the same or different phenomena? If an individual has a score on one scale that indicates high levels of satisfaction and a lower score on a different scale, should we infer that the person changed from Time 1 to Time 2, that one scale is "better" than another, or that the scales measure different cognitive states? Does better mean more sound psychometrically, closer to the "real" mental state we hope to measure, less contaminated by the individual's need to be seen as happy or unhappy (the boss may see the results of the questionnaire), that questions are more obviously related to satisfaction in the eyes of the respondent, or all of the above? Then there is the question of self-report versus observed data. Can one make a more accurate judgment about a person's level of satisfaction by asking him or her directly, or by observing manifest behavior and inferring the mental state? Does one even need to know about the mental state in order to deal with negative behaviors on the job? These are, for the moment, unanswerable questions, but they loom large in the debates to follow.

The final problem that warrants attention before the reader plunges into these debates is referred to as the *level of analysis* problem. Suppose you want to design a research study to determine the impact of boredom on both the productivity of individual workers and the performance of the company. Would an average of all workers' responses to questions about feeling bored reflect the company's BQ (boredom quotient)? Would the average of workers' performance measures represent the overall performance of the company? If we run a correlation between individual boredom responses and overall performance, a significant correlation might be an artificial result of mixed levels of analysis (individual and organizational). As another example, one might ask whether an organizational level variable such as structure should be measured by aggregating individual responses of all members of the organization to questions about structure. Is the average of all individual responses the true picture of organizational structure? Does this procedure lead to contamination of the data by perceptual differences among individuals? To compound the problem further, it is not uncommon to encounter studies in which there is substantial confusion between perceptual and objective measures of organizational characteristics. If one individual sees the organization as a monolith and another sees it in terms of the primary work group, is the average of their two judgments an accurate reflection of the real organization? Is the organization chart a more accurate reflection? Again, these are unanswerable questions, but they become important elements of the debates, especially in Chapter 5 on task design.

TOPICS OF THE DEBATES

Another important component of this introduction concerns selection of the particular topic areas of the debates. In one sense, these topics are a sampler of the major variables and concepts in organizational behavior. Each topic is, or should be, included in basic textbooks as well as advanced studies of the discipline. The debates on these topics are intended to supplement the student's understanding of these important areas. Moreover, the four debate topics (motivation, organizational behavior modification, task design and leadership) are particularly sensitive to differences of opinion at both theoretical and applied levels. Motivation, the cornerstone of the discipline, and leadership, the principal application of motivational theory, are much studied. Voluminous bodies of literature exist for each, though we have achieved less than impressive advancement in the state of our knowledge. These debates (Chapters 3 and 6, respectively) provide convincing explanations of why we have failed to make recent progress in theoretical development. At the same time, there has been enough research on these variables to enable the debators to identify their differences and offer recommendations on future direction and content of research.

The debate on organizational behavior modification has a different purpose. "OB Mod," as it is called, is a technique of analysis originally proposed by Fred Luthans and his colleagues. As a proponent in the debate, he is opposed by Pat Smith, author of a sharply critical book review. This debate provides a splendid example for those who would relish debates on the usefulness, reliability, validity and sensibleness of managerial and organizational techniques in general.

Finally, the debate on task design, Chapter 5, combines examination of an important topic area with much more general comments on the role of individual differences in designing programs for organizational improvement and a discussion of strategies for organizational research. This short chapter thus offers a triple-whammy and calls for the undivided attention of the reader.

AREAS OF DISAGREEMENT: A PREPARATION

Forewarned is forearmed! In the debates to follow a number of fundamental disagreements between the debators will crop up, sometimes two at a time. Learning theory would predict greater understanding and retention of important ideas if the reader were to go through the following sequence: a preview of areas of disagreement, contemplation of their meaning and importance, exposure to the views of experts, and a summary. The reader is then in a position to make a personal judgment on the merits or reconcilability of differing opinions. We begin with a preview of the major disagreements that will be encountered in the pages ahead.

What is science? Or more precisely, what methods of inquiry possess scientific validity and which of them are suited to the state-of-the-art in organizational behavior? On the one hand, one might argue that empirical data collection, statistical analysis, precise interpretation, and the well-controlled pitting of contradictory theoretical propositions against one another constitute true science. These procedures are "objective," replicable and quantified. The long history of theoretical development in the physical sciences attests to their usefulness. These methods appear to be necessary forerunners of applications such as the Salk vaccine, rocketry and high-yield species of corn. On the other hand, one might argue that a single case study, in-depth observation of a particular happening, is the very foundation of science. Freud, Mendel and Benjamin Franklin were masters of this art of science. Fancier words for these two approaches to science are hypothesis testing versus hypothesis generation. Which would you, the reader, use to build a theoretical model to describe or explain a mysterious element of the world around you?

The next area of disagreement revolves around the question, all things considered, would you rather be (believe) a psychologist or a sociologist (asks the editor, a psychologist)? This question brings grins to the faces of scientists from both disciplines, because we know that these stereotypes are all but meaningless in any theoretical sense. Rivalries between academic departments bearing these labels are more likely to be based on resource allocations than on disciplinary distinctions. Indeed, the boundaries between psychology and sociology grow ever more permeable. Yet there lurks beneath this question a very important issue which surfaces in the debates in many forms. This issue is the way we choose to treat individual differences in models and theories of human behavior. We know, of course, that human beings behave differently than great horned owls or aphids. We know that the sudden sight of a rattlesnake will produce a startle response in almost everybody. On the other hand, we know that acid rock music elicits very different behaviors among different individuals. What we do not know is how to find an optimal method to account for individual differences in research on the behavior of people in organizations. Do we make some assumptions about common characteristics of individuals (e.g. male, middle-aged, blue collar workers) and design work to fit these characteristics? Or do we group on the basis of intelligence? Or salary? Or need for achievement? Or do we deny these assumptions based on smaller within-group variance than between-group variance and opt for work designs that allow for maximum individualization? Closer to home, how would you assess the costs and benefits of individualized instruction versus lecture classes? From the point of view of the individual? The organization? How much you need to know about individual differences depends on your answer to these questions.

What is the nature of human behavior? This question of few words is at the heart of this book and, indeed, at the heart of the behavioral sciences. Is our behavior controlled and determined by external events (stimuli), or are we controlled by internal mental states, beliefs, needs? Some call this the ultimate chicken and egg argument and insist that it cannot be decided. Others, including your editor, believe that we must seek a fuller understanding of the elements of these differing views of human motivation, account for them in explicit research designs, and investigate the implications of both beliefs. The world of 1984 (just five years from now), brainwashing and the Skinner box are terms now used by journalists and sixth graders. But a very different view of human nature causes *passages*, psychoanalysis, self-actualization and self-expression to be the topics of cocktail party conversation. As students of human and organizational behavior, we are obliged to examine our beliefs about the nature of human motivation, to assess our own behavior toward others and the assumptions on which it rests, and to take account of these in interpreting research findings.

Abstract language, the reader charges. As a concrete and applied example, would you design a program to reduce absenteeism by attempting to change the characteristics of the work and workplace or the attitudes of workers? Would it be necessary for the workers to be consciously aware of the need for change? Would you reward good performance with bonuses or assume that good performance is its own reward? Why? Which is more ethical? Which works better? Faster?

These are issues and questions that form the central theme of the debates. One school of thought is generally described by the term *behaviorism* and its practitioners are *behaviorists*. It rests upon a philosophical premise of *behavioral determinism*. (Do consult your glossary to be sure that you understand the last two sentences.) By its nature, behaviorism focuses primarily on the prediction and control of behavior rather than causal explanation. "It works" is the practitioner's claim.

The other school of thought is called *cognitive psychology*. Conscious awareness and the human mind are at the core of this approach, and practitioners are concerned with inner or mental states, thoughts, beliefs, attitudes and values. Their claim is that cognitive theorists, unlike behaviorists, are attempting to explain, understand and develop generalizable propositions about human behavior.

In summary, the young science of organizational behavior is beset with definitional, methodological and conceptual problems. Its variables are fuzzy, its models complex. There are no universal theories or specific rules of human behavior. It is a frustrating, exciting and provocative discipline. In the pages ahead lie many questions and some answers, articulated by some of the most able scholars in the discipline in an unusual and enlightening format. As noted in the Preface, these debates were in front of a live and lively audience at the Annual Meetings of the Academy of Management - complete with laughter, groans and applause. We hope you will be glad to have joined us for this session.

REFERENCES

Pierce, J.L., and Dunham, R.B. An empirical demonstration of convergence in common macro and micro organizational measures. *Academy of Management Journal,* 1978 (in press).

Chapter 2

WHY DEBATES?

The German philosopher Hegel proposed in the 19th century that the surest path to truth is the use of dialectic, an intellectual exchange in which a thesis (statement) is pitted against an antithesis (an opposing statement). According to this principle, truth emerges from the search for synthesis of apparently contradictory views. As a very simple example, suppose you say the sky is blue, and I say it is gray. If we engage in a lively discourse, we will unearth the substance and extent of this disagreement, and the synthesis that we reach will *not* be that the sky is blue-gray, a compromise, but that we observe the sky under different conditions (I from Oregon; you from Colorado?). We are led by the dialectic process to ask ourselves and each other a sequence of questions: What is the observable nature of these differing conditions of the sky? Where can we find meteorological expertise to evaluate and test our observations? What are the implications of our findings for us and for others? Thus we resolve our apparent disagreement and are led to an enhanced understanding of our sky, our reactions to it and its effects on our own behavior and beliefs. I like blue and may wish to move to Colorado. You don't like to water your lawn and may wish to move to Oregon. Both of us will know more about the world as a result of our dialectic process, and this knowledge will permit us to make wiser decisions than if we had accepted blue-grayness or always blue or always gray as the true "state of the sky." To reach this important goal of real understanding, however, we had to invest substantial time in defining the question, seeking expertise, learning meteorological "lingo" and considering implications.

Point and Counterpoint in Organizational Behavior is a dialectic in which eight eminent scholars have made these investments on behalf of the reader and accepted the challenge to present contradictory positions, to provide the reader with raw material out of which synthesis can come. The domain, however, is not as simple as the color of the sky. The domain is human behavior, with a maze of unknown, and perhaps unknowable, elements. Our debaters will escort you to the edges of what is now known.

Why debates? Because the search for understanding, for truth, begins with identifying the questions that need to be asked. Our debators ask each other and the reader to think about what is, and what is important, and why. In so doing, each pair of debaters posits a thesis and an antithesis in their opening statements. In the Hegelian tradition, each member of the pair follows the opening statement with a response to the comments of the other and offers a summary statement to focus and clarify points of agreement and disagreement. In some of the debates, on some dimensions, debators reach a synthesis. On other dimensions, the debators agree that disagreement is appropriate, given the state of the art in organizational behavior. Our discussant, Steve Kerr, then traces a number of common themes that surface in the debates. A synthesis? In part, synthesis is provided by Professor Kerr; additional views are provided by the editor in Chapter 8. Still, the task of synthesis is incomplete. The reader is challenged to come to grips with many unresolved issues and to consider the differences in human values inherent in differences of opinion.

This book rests on the proposition that further progress, scientific and conceptual, depends on clear articulation of what is known and what needs to be known. This is the purpose of debates.

NOTES TO INSTRUCTOR AND STUDENT

Several cautions and suggestions are in order:

It is probably safe to say that each of these debaters could make a persuasive case for the opposite of his or her position. To be fair, we must once again note that the debaters have been asked to take "extreme" positions in order to highlight the areas of real and potential differences between them. All of them engaged in the original debate presentation and provided revisions for this book on the condition that they stick to these prescribed roles. Let the record be clear that they are more reasonable men and women than some of the role-prescribed statements in these pages would indicate.

Now, about the matter of personal pronouns, a subject commonly discussed in the introductions of books in recent years. His or her, he or she or s/he. You will find considerable variation among the separate chapters in this matter of personal pronouns. As your editor is a she, it was tempting to take a heavy editorial hand and remove all references to he, the manager, or he, the scholar. Yet in some of the debates there is clear intent to use he, or man, in the generic, philosophical sense. Your editor has therefore left a number of such usages intact and invites the reader to accept them accordingly.

Some suggestions are in order on the use of debates in the classroom, as an aid to learning and retention of concepts in organizational behavior. The list of potential debate topics is as long as the list of topics in OB. As earlier noted, the discipline is in its conceptual infancy and thus ripe for the use of dialectic in working through contradictory research findings and tentative models of human behavior. The following two examples will demonstate this point:

Management by Objectives (MBO) programs have become a widespread, some would even say endemic, practice in modern organizations. The search for accountability and increased productivity in private and public organizations has triggered a "results orientation," with consequent attention to organization-wide programs. Such programs are labeled in a variety of ways and vary in their intensiveness, effectiveness and completeness.

Most graduates of schools of business or adminstration will encounter some variation on the MBO theme in their first jobs. Some may even be asked to evaluate these programs. (You just graduated from a business school, didn't you? Well, are MBO programs any good?) What better basis for dealing with such questions than participation in a *research-based* debate as a part of the OB course? In this author's experience, no other teaching technique is so likely to cause high levels of student involvement, full investigation into the available evidence, or airing of important issues and concerns about MBO. Will a debate answer the question, "Are MBO programs any good?" Clearly not. But listening to a statement of pro and con positions, with appropriate qualifiers, is a very productive experience. Try it, you will like it — but you will work very much harder at it than when the instructor speaks and the student passively records.

A second example: Any OB course which encourages discussion comes sooner or later to the question, "How are satisfaction and performance related, or are they, or can they be?" Most students (and other people) have an intuitive sense that these two variables, as we call them scientifically, are related. There is a growing list of articles and books written on this subject which provides rich fodder for development of a classroom debate. Will there be a winner in such a debate? No, no more than there will be a winner in the debates to follow in this book. The processes of identifying areas of agreement and disagreement, searching for conditional properties and surfacing inherent personal values, however, *are* education. Instructor, take heed. Don't let student debates end in easy compromises. MBO and the satisfaction-performance relationship are not blue-gray any more than the sky is.

Finally, some pedagogical advice for readers of this book and prospective classroom debators: The reach for synthesis and understanding will be facilitated by taking time to work through several questions at the end of each debate. The reader, student and instructor should allocate time and conceptual energy for this process.

a) On what issues are the debators in agreement?

b) On what issues are the debators in disagreement?

c) Under what conditions might contradictory positions be reconciled?

d) Which of the areas of disagreement seem to rest on fundamental differences in personal values, beliefs about the nature of man?

e) Do your own personal values cause you to evaluate one position as being more legitimate or valid than the other? (There is nothing wrong with a yes answer to this question, but it is nonetheless an important one to face up to.)

f) Which of the areas of disagreement seem to result from insufficient empirical evidence, inappropriate research designs, inadequate definition of terms, or all three?

g) What can be done to remedy these insufficiencies?

h) In the meantime, how can I make effective use of the contents of the debate in making my own behavioral decisions?

Part II

THE DEBATES

CHAPTER 3   Motivation
CHAPTER 4   Organizational Behavior Modification
CHAPTER 5   Task Design
CHAPTER 6   Leadership

Chapter 3

MOTIVATION

INTRODUCTION

Brace yourself! This first debate may be tough going. But have patience and persevere; you will be richly rewarded for your efforts.

There are several reasons why this debate makes difficult reading: Professors Locke and Hamner are terribly bright; they are thoroughly familiar with each other's positions; and they have eloquent command of both technical and nontechnical uses of the English language. You will learn, as I have with pleasure, that their well-turned phrases convey precise thoughts if one works through to the core. They are not, as sometimes happens in academic writing, guilty of overcomplicating simple material. Their language is complex because they are presenting complex ideas. Besides, if you have never heard of an epiphenomenon, it's high time.

If you are a beginner in the discipline of organizational behavior and psychology, let me assist you by providing a framework and introducing some technical terms and concepts you will encounter in this debate. The central theme of this debate, indeed of this book, is an apparent dichotomy between behavioristic psychologists and cognitive psychologists. As noted in Chapter 1, this dichotomy may be more apparent than real, but its implications unquestionably influence the design, conduct and results of present-day research in organizational behavior. Nowhere is this more evident than in the study of a variable called motivation, the foundation on which the discipline of organizational behavior is built. What is this thing called motivation? For one, it is the study of human behavior, action. Why do people do what they do, think as they think, believe as they believe? Why do we go to war or seek peace, have friends or enemies, work or play, strive or loll about, achieve or resign? In this sense, the study of motivation is the study of verbs, action verbs. By comparison, the study of organizational design or structure is the study of nouns, words that describe things or states.

In another, more narrow sense, motivation involves changing the behavior of self and others. If it is difficult to understand behavior as it occurs naturally, it is even more difficult to understand, predict and control the process of changing behavior. Note, unwary reader, that changing is a *process*. This implies sequence, a time dimension, and relationships of several kinds. These relationships include before-after, person-environment, self-other, individual-group, feelings-thoughts, acts-rewards, cause-effect and variations and combinations of these and others. The debate on motivation brushes all of these; hence you will find the debate a rich source of food-for-thought about who you are, why you act in certain ways, and what you can do about misbehavior.

As you read the debate, watch for some basic dilemmas the debaters pose: Is a theory of motivation that is based on reinforcement principles better because "it works"? Does it work? When does it work? Why does it work? Is a cognitive approach superior because it seeks to explain and understand the *causes* of behavior? Should the proof of the pudding, the test of superiority, be logical soundness, statistical regularity, ability to get results, manageability? Is either of these more "scientific" than the other? Less? This debate, or this book, will not answer the question "What is science?" but it will certainly point out that legitimate differences of opinion exist and that these differences are clearly reflected in the way we set out to get answers to questions, i.e., do research.

For example, let us undertake an analysis of the motives which lead you to read this book. We could ask you to reflect upon (introspect) and report to us the three or four most important reasons. These motives might be intrinsic (I want to learn), extrinsic (it was assigned), instrumental (I want to get a good grade in the course), valent (I like it), activating (I wanted something to do), dissonance-reducing (I'm paying good money for my education), equity-producing (the instructor thinks I am a good student) or any of many others. Using this approach to analysis, reflect-and-report, we would be focusing on your perceived needs, a thoroughly cognitive approach. The data you supply, the list of reasons or motives as you perceive them, would be the basis for our interpretation of your cognitive needs and, in comparison with responses from others and analysis of other activities in which you engage, would form the basis for understanding your cognitive "map" of the world. This knowledge of your cognitions might aid us in convincing you to read the book.

Or perhaps we should take a different tack. What if we observe, over a period of time, the environmental conditions which are associated with your decision to read a textbook. Elective or required course? Graded or ungraded? Optional or required reading? Paperback or hardcover? Green or blue? Large print or small? Easy or hard? Good performance or poor performance in the course? Other courses? What rewards seem to "turn you on"? And many more questions. The data in this case would be observations of historical behavior. Our knowledge of these data might assist us in arranging environmental circumstances such that there would be a high probability of your reading this book. We would be using a reinforcement or behavioristic approach.

Now stop and think for a moment about the differences between these two approaches, the problems with each. NO! *Really* stop and think. Write down some of these problems. Now, read on.

If we add to the complexity of the research problem in this one case for one person by adding questions about other people/students and other activities beside reading textbooks, we begin to multiply the conceptual, analytical and interpretive problems. If we find tentatively acceptable solutions to these problems and proceed to collect and interpret data, we are likely to feel we should propose a "theory" to explain textbook-reading behavior. If we wish to test that theory by experimentation, would we manipulate (experimentally change) the environmental characteristics (e.g., reward system) or the perceived needs of individuals? Would our primary interest be in trying to predict and control your reading behavior, or in trying to explain *why* you, personally, decided to read, or not to read, a textbook? Or both?

Now, with these questions in mind and a humble acknowledgment that there are no easy answers, let us turn to the experts. Remember, please, that they have been asked to take "extreme" positions. Our task (and theirs, *after* the debate) is to search for areas of compatibility, to attempt to resolve inconsistencies, or at least to identify specific areas of real and insoluble differences between cognitive and behavioristic models.

Resolved: Attitudes and cognitive processes are necessary elements in motivational models.

Barbara Karmel: Our speaker for the affirmative of this resolution is Edwin A. Locke and for the negative is W. Clay Hamner.

Ed Locke: Let me begin by reversing the question posed in the resolution. Let us consider the implications of the premise that cognition (i.e., the mind) is *not* relevant to motivation. One possible inference is that man has no mind. Such a conclusion would be obviously self-contradictory since any argument offered to refute the mind would require the existence of a (reasoning) mind.

A second, more generally held view, is that man has a mind but it is a useless epiphenomenon with no causal efficacy, that it is merely an incidental by-product of man's biological functioning and/or

EDWIN A. LOCKE

Edwin A. Locke is Professor of Business and Management, and of Psychology, at the University of Maryland. Holding his Ph.D. in Industrial Psychology from Cornell University, Dr. Locke's major research has been in the areas of job satisfaction, enrichment and motivation.

He has contributed numerous articles to the *Journal of Applied Psychology*, the *American Psychologist*, *Psychological Reports*, *Organizational Behavior and Human Performance*, and many others. He is a consulting editor of *Journal of Applied Psychology*.

Dr. Locke is a fellow of the American Psychological Association and a member of the Maryland Psychological Association, the Biofeedback Society, the New York Academy of Sciences, the Society for Organizational Behavior, and the Academy of Management.

environmental conditioning. This view implies that men's behavior is simply a function of their drives and their wives. (I don't have a parallel statement for women, because I couldn't find a word that rhymes with husbands.)

One could argue that according to epiphenomenalism, mental actions hold approximately the same status as dreams. In a dream state the individual is not aware of the outside world and is not directing his thoughts or actions. Cognitive activity is not purposeful but passive, the result of random associations among prior experiences. Dreams are seeming epiphenomena of brain activity during sleep. For the behaviorist, this is equally true of man when he is awake, not by choice (for a person can choose to walk around in a dazed stupor) but by his very nature.

What is the behaviorist's proof of the view that man's mind is simply an epiphenomenon, that it has no causal efficacy, no effect on what he believes or does? Interestingly, if one reads the behaviorist literature one can find no proof whatever of this claim. Skinner (1953, p. 9), for example, admits that environmental determinism (a doctrine which implies epiphenomenalism) is simply an *assumption*. Behaviorists talk constantly about the development of "laws" which will demonstrate causal linkages between stimuli, responses (behavior) and reinforcements, but if one looks at the evidence one finds that *no such laws have been discovered*. The alleged law of reinforcement refers to nothing more than demonstrations that rewards result in an increased frequency of responding under certain conditions (which conditions have never been fully identified by the behaviorists).

Skinner (1953) acknowledges that when he talks of causal laws he means the establishment of functional (statistical) relationships between response rate and reinforcement schedule, *not* the identification of necessary and sufficient conditions to explain behavioral response. While these functional relationships are established by the experimental method, they do not prove that the reinforcement alone causes (necessitates) the change in response frequency. It is a fallacy to assume that because one has manipulated only one variable in an experiment that therefore only one variable is needed to explain the effects.

Consider the following example. Suppose a computer operator presses the "start" button and then observes the computer print out the answer to a problem. Suppose further that this "stimulus-response" relationship occurred regularly. Certainly no one would conclude from this that pushing the "start" button was in itself the cause of the computer's problem-solving activity. A full explanation would require an identification of the computer's physical structure, its power source, its programming and the data input. Pushing the "start" button is a necessary condition, but it is only a sufficient condition for solving the problem *in a specific context,* i.e., when the other necessary elements are present. With respect to man the issue is even more complex. Unlike a computer, a man can choose to turn his power — his mind — on and off, can program himself, and can question his own programming. Furthermore, his internal "structure" is not just physical but includes consciousness.

Now consider the effects of reinforcement. Even some prominent behaviorists now admit that reinforcement is *not* necessary for learning (Herrnstein, 1977), although they do assert that it is necessary for performance. However, in order to defend the latter assertion behaviorists have been forced to acknowledge that not all reinforcement is from the external environment. This increasingly prevalent retreat into concepts such as "self-reinforcement" (e.g., Mahoney, 1974) is an implicit admission of the causal efficacy of the mind and an implicit contradiction of the premise of environmental determinism.

Reinforcement may be a sufficient condition for behavior change, but again, only in a specific context. These contextual factors (identified by cognitive psychologists) would seem to include (as a minimum): (a) some degree of awareness on the part of the individual as to how to get the reinforcement (or at least an hypothesis about how to get it); and (b) a need or desire for the reinforcement (Brewer, 1974; Dulany, 1968). Both sets of conditions refer to states and actions of consciousness.

In practice, behavior modification often works precisely because behaviorists try to insure that the subject *knows* how to get reinforced, e.g., by telling him how or by presenting the reinforcer right after the correct behavior, and because they typically use something which the subject is known to *value* as a reinforcer. Unfortunately, the implications of these practices have never been accounted for in the behaviorist philosophy.

It is not necessary, however, to cite laboratory experiments in order to demonstrate the fallacy of environmental determinism. The evidence that man possesses volition is available through introspection, by thinking about it. Rand (1964) has pointed out that man's basic psychological freedom involves the choice to think or not to think. Anyone can observe by introspection that he can choose to focus his mind, that he can set it to the task of integrating, of question-asking, of evaluating, of criticizing, of identifying and resolving contradictions, of searching for implications, of looking for deeper explanations, of pursuing the answers to questions across a period of time. It must be stressed that the choice to think is not uncaused or random. It is caused by man.

One can also attack determinism from the negative side, by showing that the denial of the premise that man can choose to think leads to self-contradiction (Locke, 1966, 1969). For example, a consistent behaviorist who was giving a talk on his theories would have to admit, "I'm up here presenting my views, but the reason I am expressing them has nothing to do with my beliefs. I've just been conditioned to emit these word sounds. They are not caused by my ideas; they're just things I was compelled to say. I can't help it. I was forced to spout behaviorism and determinism by my environmental conditioning." Well, a behaviorist is free to say this, but then we need not consider his views any further because he's confessing that he's a robot and is simply programmed to babble in a certain way. If he is not a rational being, he can't help what he says and can't validate his knowledge.

The basic philosophical premise of behaviorism is, therefore, false according to the evidence of introspection and logic. So if it's false, what would be the requirements of a rational model of motivation. The four basic motivational concepts, in my opinion, are: (1) the concept of needs — the objective requirements of man's mental and physical health and well-being; (2) the concept of values — what man seeks to gain or keep, his acquired conscious or subconscious conceptions of the good or the beneficial; (3) the concept of goals — his particular aims and objectives, and (4) emotions — the form in which he experiences value judgements.

Even these four concepts, however, would not be adequate to account for man's choices and actions without including consideration of man's

W. CLAY HAMNER

W. Clay Hamner is currently Professor of Organizational Behavior at Duke University. He received his doctorate in organizational behavior from Indiana University, and is a member of the Academy of Management and the American Psychological Association.

Dr. Hamner has published over 30 articles on motivational principles and applications in such periodicals as the *Journal of Personality and Social Psychology, Journal of Applied Psychology, Journal of Experimental Social Psychology, Organizational Behavior and Human Performance, Sociometry* and *Behavioral Science.* He is the coauthor of three textbooks: *Contemporary Problems in Personnel* (St. Clair Press, 1974, 1977); *Organizational Behavior and Management: A Contingency Approach* (St. Clair Press, 1974, 1977); and *Organizational Behavior: An Applied Psychological Approach* (Business Publications, Inc., 1978).

distinctive mode of cognition. Man is a rational being. This means that he has the *capacity* to reason, to integrate and identify the material provided by his sense organs (Rand, 1964). It is reason which gives man the capacity to identify the nature of his needs and discover how to satisfy them; to choose values that will further his happiness and well being; to set appropriate goals; and to identify and understand (and, if necessary, change) his emotions. Reason, however, as noted earlier, is a faculty that one uses by choice; it is volitional. A man who does not choose to think will seem to be the helpless victim of his environment; he will not choose rational values or set reasonable goals or have rational emotions or satisfy his needs. Such a man will be pushed and pulled in every direction, riddled with conflicts and self-doubts and easily swayed by outside forces. Such a man, however, would represent the essence not of human nature but rather of human pathology. And even pathological behavior cannot be explained except by reference to pathological mental contents and processes.

Clay Hamner: It will come as no surprise to hear that my position is different from that of Professor Locke on many points. Before I outline these differences, let me make one point perfectly clear. *All theories of motivation contain what we commonly label as cognitions.* These cognitive components are given different names by different theories: for example, awareness (developmental theory), public knowledge (reinforcement theory), tacting (reinforcement theory), origin (cognitive evaluation theory), internal control (personality theory), self-denial (hedonistic theory), no-trial learning (learning theory), self-reward (behavior modification theory), significant others (field theory), values (expectancy theory), social comparison (equity theory, attribution theory) and intentions (goal-setting theory).

As I mentioned, even reinforcement theory, which Ed apparently feels is as close to "bad" as a theory with empirical support can be, contains many references to cognitive states. A close reading of Skinner (1969, pp. vii-xii) and Bandura (1969, 1976) will reveal the importance of the cognitive states of awareness, a person's need state (satiation level), the intrinsic enjoyment of a task, and self-control and feedback to reinforcement theory.

The major disagreement, therefore, is not whether or not a person has a *mind* which processes cognitive information from the environment when determining which behavior is appropriate. The mind *is* an important component of behavior. We know that people who are "aware" of the relationship between their behavior and the consequences of behavior are better prepared to respond appropriately to their environment than people whose prior experiences have been below their threshold of awareness. We know that people who are able to store the rules of "discrimination" and "generalization" in their minds are better able to respond to novel environments than individuals whose mental capacity is such that each time they enter novel environments they must enter into search behavior until the environment reconditions them. In addition, a person who possesses public knowledge, that is, the ability to describe correctly the relationship of his behavior to the outcome he experiences, is able to respond faster and is also able to use his verbal skills to help others respond in a manner that will lead to the desired results. Moreover, I believe, as do most reinforcement proponents, that people whose rewards come from themselves or from a neutral environment have a more positive attitude toward their environments, tasks, and rewards than do those who must depend on a judgment made by a third person who cognitively interprets whether or not the response was appropriate.

To this point, therefore, I have not disagreed with the contention that internal states in one's mind have an impact on one's behavioral response. What, then, are my points of disagreement with the arguments presented by Professor Locke? My first disagreement with Professor Locke centers on whether or not attitudes and cognitions are *necessary* components of theories of motivation. My contention is that they are not. Researchers have been able to predict behavior successfully by studying the environment and the reinforcing consequences of various behaviors within that environment. It is not argued that attitudes and other cognitive processes do not exist, but instead, that they are *outcomes* or *results* of behavior and not *causes* of behavior. Bem (1967), for example, has long argued and gathered empirical evidence to support the contention that a person who wants to "know" his or her feelings or beliefs must study his or her own behavior and, in essence, ask, "What must my attitude be if I behave in this fashion in this situation?" (Why did I run? Was it because I was afraid?) Therefore, since cognitions are discovered from one's behaviors (i.e., I become "aware," I discover "pleasure," I "enjoy," and so forth), then it seems that cognitions result from one's experience in an environment. If one wants to change a cognition, one must change the behavior which led to its discovery. Indeed, the contingencies of reinforcement (i.e., the environment and the consequences of the behavior in that environment) are necessary components of a theory of behavior *and* a theory of cognitive processes.

Nevertheless, research has shown that public knowledge of the contingencies of reinforcement can cause higher levels of performance than private knowledge of the same contingencies. Therefore, a person's mental processes are very important. We must understand, however, that it is the *contingencies* and not the cognitions which *caused* the behavior.

My second disagreement with Professor Locke centers on a different version of the question we are debating. I would not be opposed to a logical argument by Professor Locke that cognitions are necessary components in motivational models. However, those of you who have paid close attention to his arguments know he has been arguing that "attitudes and cognitions are *sufficient* elements in motivational models." They simply are not. Even abnormal psychologists (meaning psychologists who study abnormal behavior) and psychiatrists invest a great deal of time in the introspection process attempting to get the client to examine and understand his own past reinforcement history and the various environments he has experienced.

To argue that cognitions are sufficient elements in a motivational model makes the flagrant assumption that cognitions are the origin of behavior rather than meditating variables between the environment and the behavior.[1] Professor Locke has accused reinforcement theorists of denying the cognitive aspect of man, which they do not; he at the same time denies the existence of the environment as a causal element of behavior. The origin of behavior is the environment of man. This is not to say that man cannot act on his environment, or choose to move to a more pleasant environment; it is only to say that man's

---

[1]Whereas reinforcement theory says that cognitions are learned or discovered and therefore are outcome (dependent) variables rather than meditating (independent) variables, it does not deny their existence or importance.

self is not separate from the environment he is currently experiencing or the ones he has previously experienced.

My third disagreement with Professor Locke follows from the previous point. What are the various determinants of behavior, and which ones do managers control? Apparently for Professor Locke they are "values," "emotions" and "intentions." All three are cognitive in origin and, according to Professor Locke, can be examined through introspection. Professor Locke seems to be confused about the issue over which we are debating. Ed, this debate is not about introspection. We are not trying to teach a "know thyself" doctrine. We are concerned with the much more practical issue of developing motivational models to help managers in organizations understand how their behavior can positively influence their subordinates' productivity. Therefore, a model of motivation should describe what a manager controls that will energize behavior, channel behavior toward the desired level of performance, and maintain that level of performance over time (e.g., see Hamner and Organ, 1978, pp. 137-162). The introspection should come on the part of the manager (motivator) rather than on the part of the subordinate. He should ask himself, "What is it I control that will have a beneficial effect on the productivity and satisfaction of my employees?"

If a manager were to ask himself, for example, why there is a high turnover rate among his employees, he would find a multitude of motives (causes) for people quitting their jobs. If he were to classify these reasons into categories, he would probably find three categories of reasons. *First,* some people might quit because of the environment created by the manager. Either the climate in terms of support, goal clarity or physical surroundings was negative; the task assigned was a negative or dull one; the rewards were too low; or the rewards were not viewed as being contingently administered. *Second,* some people might quit because of conditions created by the environment external to the manager. They had a better job opportunity, their family wanted to move to a better climate, the economy caused a fear of a job loss and so forth. *Third,* for the sake of argument, let's assume that some people might quit because of various values, needs, emotions, intentions, attitudes and other cognitions that they have learned from the internal work environment or the environment as a whole and which are incompatible with their present employment.

If we suppose that all three of these categories have uniquely or jointly contributed to the employees' motives for quitting, where should the manager concentrate his efforts, Ed? I suggest that the manager should concentrate his efforts on those things he controls directly, such as task designs, job assignments, job matching, creating a pleasant work environment, freedom of movement, contingent pay, and so forth. He should *not* concentrate his efforts on trying to change the whole world or trying to use God-like introspection to change the interworkings of the employees' minds. The latter two strategies are useless and even dangerous, both in terms of a low probability of success and a high probability of failure. In fact, I contend he would have a much better chance of impacting the global environment and the individual's cognitive map by manipulating those variables he is perceived to control legitimately. The job is his business; employees' minds are not.

The fourth thing which we seem to disagree on is the concept of a motivational model. I have this uneasy feeling (I discovered it while you were talking) that we are clear on our definitions of attitudes and cognitions but not on our definition of motivational models. When I talk about motivational models, I am talking about models which managers can use to develop a philosophy of management based on an understanding of what makes "normal" (as compared to abnormal or inconsistent) people act and react in a voluntary (free choice) work environment. In your discussion of motivation, I cannot put my hands on anything that a manager or any other second party can use to increase the productivity of another person or persons. It seems you have been discussing how a person can better understand what makes him behave the way he does. Great. I believe in self-examination. I'm all for self-analysis. It can be healthy and useful. I'd rather be "maze bright" than "maze dull" (see Jennings, 1971), especially when it is my own maze. Nevertheless, the goal of the behavioral scientist should be to examine (measure), explain, influence and predict the behavior of others as well as his own behavior. I'm not sure your kind of motivational model has much practical value for the outside party who is not privy to the introspection process.

I think it is important that we as organizational behaviorists avoid confusing scientific curiosity with self-analysis. As scientists we have two kinds of hats to wear. First, based on inductive or deductive logic, we wear hats as theory builders so that we can develop a useful body of knowledge for others. Second, we need to put on empirical hats and examine our theories and those of others to see where the theories hold and where they should be modified. The latter role assumes we can detach ourselves from our theories.

As both scientists and human beings we are preoccupied with understanding ourselves. This is why we find the popular-press self-analysis books interesting, entertaining and even informative. While we have a right and an obligation to test the theories espoused in the lay press when their prescriptions and our own theories touch on the same problems, we should be very careful not to accept on "faith" the teachings or tenets of the cult press because of our emotional involvement. If we do, we compromise our roles as scientists. I fear that any body of knowledge based on introspection, abnormal psychology theories and the popular-press prescriptions can do more harm than good to our progress as scientists unless we are willing to test empirically before we make prescriptive statements. For example, I would warn any reader of this debate not to accept on faith either of the extreme arguments being presented here. Rather, be a critic of both positions.

My last point of disagreement with Professor Locke is probably the one about which I feel most strongly. I am willing to entertain the possibility that attitudes and cognitions explain performance. That is, while I think the external environment is a strong determinant of behavior, I am willing to examine my position scientifically to see if it holds. If it doesn't, I'm willing to modify my position. I don't believe Professor Locke is as willing to examine his theoretical position with empirical tests. I can hear you thinking, "What are you talking about? Professor Locke has published over 30 laboratory studies showing the relationship between goals and performance." The problem is that these studies are not a sufficient test of his theory, the cognitive view. He has *not* accounted for the possibility of alternative explanations, specifically, behavioristic interpretations of his results. He has *not* designed research to test competing behavioristic hypotheses. However, it is only fair to point out that Professor Locke is not alone in making this error. As I have argued elsewhere (see Hamner, Ross and Staw, 1978), organizational researchers appear to be garrisoned in different "camps," with scant inclination to consider the views being advanced by others. There is always the hazard that an individual researcher's attachment to his own formulations will produce bias in his research. His theoretical stance frames his view of the world, determines to a degree how research is designed, and has an impact on how research results are interpreted. Using a set of consistent, noncompeting, unchallenged assumptions about motivation may lead to the undermining of research even before the design stage is reached or the hypothesis encountered. Such an approach is hardly conducive to progress in the field.

What I am contending is that the results of studies in organizational behavior are often misleading. There are several possible causes. Results can be misleading due to artifacts in the research itself, or they can be misleading because statistically significant relationships do not *explain* the theoretically independent variance of performance and satisfaction. The researcher may have chosen to measure environmental perceptions as an estimate of environmental determinants of outcomes, when he or she would have been able to explain at least the same amount of variance (that is, the same data set overlap), and perhaps more variance, had an historical predictor rather than an ahistorical predictor been used. Research results may also be artificial because the researcher bases his or her argument on perceptual dependent variables as well as perceptual independent variables. The cognitive dissonance literature would predict that the individual's need to demonstrate consistency predetermines that these perceptions would be highly correlated. Furthermore, a critical examination of the recent research by Deci (see Hamner and Foster, 1975) and Latham (see Kim and Hamner, 1976) supports my charge that some researchers are prone to make the data "fit" the theory rather than the theory fit the data.

What, then, would be a sufficient test of a theory which would lead to progress in the field? Both Ed and I need to do several things to settle our disagreements and to make progress as scientists. Each of us has advanced a theoretical position which focuses on one primary antecedent (either the environment or an internal state) of current or future behavior. As it currently exists, the research process is one of theory advocacy or criticism: our general research paradigm is such that data either support or refute our hypotheses, but rarely are the hypotheses framed to test more than one of the theories at a time. Unfortunately, our consideration of one motivational approach at a time may be doing a grave disservice to both theory development and practical application. In short, we must seriously ask whether our theories of motivation are truly contradictory or have the potential for integration.

Our challenge now is to integrate the competing antecedents into alternative research designs in such a way that we do two things. *First,* we need to examine the amount of *unique* variance explained by each of the antecedents. For example, a recent study by Hamner, Mainstone and Ross (1976) found that by combining environmental, expectancy and individual-difference variables, twice as much variance could be explained as compared to the variance any one set of predictive variables alone could explain.

Second, we need to test rival hypotheses generated by the various theories. It is impossible to prove or disprove a theory if we refuse to test the alternative explanations of that theory. While our theories may *seem* to be well thought out and deductively sound, as social scientists we have failed miserably in the task of designing fair and unbiased tests of our theories. Even though there are hundreds of studies which supposedly support each theory of motivation, very few studies test rival hypotheses. We seem to hide from the truth rather than discover the truth when we use this as our model of research.

We not only hide from the truth by refusing to examine a theory against competing explanations, but some cognitive theorists even claim that we cannot discover the true causes of behavior, because we don't possess sufficient skills as scientists. For example, Deci (1975, pp.7,8) says:

Consider this example: A person happens to look down one day and finds a $10 bill on the street. After that, he spends more time looking down. A behavioristic interpretation of this behavior would be that the response of looking down was reinforced by the $10 — with the result that the response recurs more frequently. The person does not *decide* to do it; it happens because of the strengthening of associations between stimuli (e.g., presence of the street, etc.) and the response (i.e., looking down). A cognitive interpretation, on the other hand, would be that the person values money, and he decides, because of finding the $10, that he may find money more often if he looks down more. So he decides to look down more, and the behavior follows the decision. The data can help to substantiate either theory, but they cannot prove that a person's decisions affect, or do not affect his behavior. They do not really give us the essence of the answers to why the person looks down more.

So, experimental data help us build theories and derive comprehensive frameworks to account for behavior. And, indeed, this is the goal of scientific psychology, to be able to account for behavior in a comprehensive and systematic way. The goal is not, as people often think, to discover ultimate truths about what makes humans work. Those ultimate truths are not discoverable, they are only assumable.

I disagree. While we may be a long way from discovering the truth about what makes humans work, we must avoid the temptation to forgo truth because we do not yet know it or because we fear that by discovering it we would have to alter our own view of the world.

It would seem at this juncture that Ed and I, between us, have identified many of the variables that must be considered in predicting and understanding human behavior in the world of work. What is now necessary is to gauge their respective importance and set about the task of improving our total predictive capabilities. In the past our environment has rewarded isolated investigations. Reward systems in our environment have led us to assume that such specific, single-theory investigations constitute a valued outcome. I propose that we establish an increase in predictive capabilities as our goal and work to achieve this goal through the use of integrated approaches to the study of human motivation.

Ed Locke: Clay, of course I cannot disagree with your position that the science of human behavior has not yet developed its full potential for theory-testing research. A major cause of this unfortunate situation, I believe, is the philosophy of behaviorism, which has pushed us in the wrong direction with respect to the status of the mind in psychology.

I would like to point out, Clay, that you even contradict yourself regarding the causal status of cognitions. In several places you assert that cognitions are "important," that they "have an impact on a person's behavioral response," that they are "necessary" components in motivational models. On the other hand, you claim, in agreement with Skinner, that cognitions are epiphenomena, that "they are *outcomes* or *results* of behavior and not *causes* of behavior." Which is it, Clay? You can't have it both ways.

Clay claims that I misunderstand the subject of the debate. I think he does. The resolution in this debate involves the role of cognitions in "motivational models," not in practical applications. All models, however, have practical implications, including cognitive models. The manager who accepts a cognitive model can and does use it in numerous ways: i.e., in the selection of employees (with the appropriate values), in making performance appraisals, in diagnosing performance and morale problems, in determining job assignments. A manager does not necessarily have to change an employee's values in order to take account of them, although he will frequently attempt to influence goals.

As to the issue of submitting our ideas to empirical test, I do not agree that it would resolve the disagreements. The reason is that our disagreements are not fundamentally scientific but philosophical. They *precede* rather than follow empirical research. The philosophical issues must be decided by logic rather than by experiment.

Our obvious area of disagreement clearly centers on the following issue: What is the ultimate *cause* of human action? This presupposes an answer to the question: What constitutes an *explanation* of human action? I agree with Rand's neo-Aristolelian view that finding answers to these questions requires one to identify the attributes and characteristics of the entity which is acting (Locke, 1972). All actions are actions of some particular entity. Every entity has a specific nature, i.e., particular characteristics. These determine what it can do and will do in a particular situation.

Man is an entity of a particular type. Most fundamentally, he is a conceptual being. His mind is his means of survival, the tool by which he guides his choices and actions. Without reference to his mind (e.g., his beliefs, goals, values, mental processes etc.) *no* explanation of his actions is possible (Locke, 1972).

Let me illustrate this point. For years, studies have demonstrated that there is a functional (stimulus-response) relationship between feedback (or knowledge of results) and efficient or improved task performance. But what can we conclude from these studies? Feedback causes or conditions performance improvement? No, because a functional relationship (correlation) is not a statement of causality. The proof is that this relationship does not always hold (Locke, Cartledge and Koeppel, 1968).

Early feedback researchers failed to look at the attributes and characteristics of the human beings given the feedback.

Specifically they failed to identify the mental process which caused the feedback to be translated into improved performance, e.g., such processes as perception, appraisal and goal-setting. Subsequent cognitively based research found that while feedback might be a necessary condition for improved task performance, it was not a sufficient condition (Locke, Cartledge and Koeppel, 1968). The sufficient (and necessary) conditions include mental processes. Identifying these processes allows us to *explain* how feedback improves performance. The functional relationship, in and of itself, tells us little or nothing.

I would argue that the environment *by itself* is not sufficient to explain *any* human behavior (even though it is a necessary element in any full philosophical explanation, since man does not exist in a vacuum). S-R laws are not even sufficient to explain sense-perception. Perception cannot occur unless objects in the environment are attended to, the sensory input is above threshold, and the input is processed by the brain, so that it gives rise to awareness. To explain more complex human activity, one has to know not only how environment is perceived, but also what knowledge or beliefs the individual has about it; how he appraises it, based on his values; what conclusions he reaches; what goals he sets; his self-concept. Based on the environment alone, one cannot *know* the answer to these questions. One can observe similarities, patterns, or statistical regularities, but these are not explanations.

In conclusion, I would like to mention a brilliant and fascinating two-volume work which I read recently entitled *The Criminal Personality* (Yochelson and Samenow, 1976/1977). Based on the results of this study, which was probably the most thorough and painstaking investigation of criminals ever conducted, the authors concluded that criminal behavior could not be explained as a result of a bad environment (e.g., criminals were not rejected by their parents; rather, the parents were rejected by the criminals). Nor could the behavior of criminals be permanently changed by environmental manipulations. Yochelson and Samenow found that the criminals' behavior was caused by 52 types of thinking errors which were manifested by every member of their sample; furthermore, they discovered that criminality could be cured only by totally eliminating these criminal thought patterns and replacing them with more responsible cognitive habits. The acquisition and elimination of these thought patterns was a matter of the criminal's own choice.

Criminals have always been considered the archetype of the determined personality, creatures of their environments, so if it is the case that they have free will, how can you argue that we don't?

Clay Hamner: Ed, your argument leads to the conclusion that we are all criminals. Surely you are not confusing the work of Yochelson and Samenow with empirical work — or for that matter making a comparison between criminal behavior and voluntary work behavior. And even more surely, you would not carry your argument further and say such things as:

People are poor because they choose to be poor;

People are not rich because they inherit money; they are rich because they choose to be rich;

Blacks aren't discriminated against by whites because whites are biased; blacks choose to be discriminated against.

Your argument sounds more like a belief in "predestination" than in "free will." A reading of *Beyond Freedom and Dignity* by Skinner (1971) surely would not lead one to conclude that a belief in the environment as the historical cause of behavior is contrary to the belief in free will.

There are several comments which need to be made about your theses that the "environment psychologically explains *no* variance in human behavior whatsoever," and "introspection proves the philosophical premise of behaviorism false" (and therefore, I assume, your cognitive theory true). If introspection is the only way to test your theory, why does your research use pooled variance to explain behavior? Why don't you study one person at a time? Pooled variance could never be used to explain the mind, and therefore any empirical research which uses more than one subject, according to your logic, could not explain anything. Second, your argument that the environment explains *no* variance is as ludicrous as the argument by Watson (1924), p. 24, who said;

Give me a dozen healthy infants, well formed, and my own specified world to bring them up in and I'll guarantee to take any one at random and train him to become any type of specialist I might select — doctor, lawyer, merchant-chief, and yes, even beggar-man and thief, regardless of his talents, penchants, tendencies, abilities, vocations, and race of his ancestors.

A close reading of any good developmental psychology text would be able to refute either extreme position.

Third, if you refuse to measure the environment, how can you possibly know whether or not it can predict, influence or explain behavior. *Most cognitive studies clearly show that the environment explains nothing more than random error variance. Likewise, most reinforcement studies clearly show that the internal states of man explain nothing more than random error variance.* Both results are statistically correct. What we're calling random error variance in many cases is not random at all. It's random error by choice of the researcher and not by the results themselves. If one class of independent variables were manipulated and a second class were treated as random occurrence, you would not expect to find support for the latter class. Statistically you can't lose. However, the finding of statistical support for one school of thought does not refute the other school of thought; nor does it mean that by combining the two classes of variables *additional unique variance* would not be explained.

Fourth, Ed, I don't know if you are talking about self-knowledge, that is, motivation of the self, or motivation of others. I can't deny that introspection is important for self-knowledge. But I deny that managers have a right to involve themselves in a clinical practice of psychology when it comes to motivating, getting inside the head of, other people in a voluntary work setting.

Ed, I have this terrible feeling that you are using the religious argument of "faith" to substitute for empirical support of your position. You really can't expect people to blindly accept your position because you have, through some introspective process, been to the mountain. Like Saul on the road to Damascus, I feel faith is not enough, show me a sign.

Ed Locke: Clay, you claim that I would *not* claim that people are poor because they choose to be poor, or rich because they choose to be rich. You are right; I would not. However, I would say that certain people choose courses of action and philosophies of life (often subconsciously) that make these outcomes more or less likely.

Clay, you also claim that "a reading of *Beyond Freedom and Dignity* by Skinner (1971) surely would not lead one to conclude that a belief that the environment is the historical cause of behavior is contrary to the belief of free will." Yes, it would. In fact, to destroy the concept of free will once and for all was one of Skinner's purposes in writing that book.

When I say the environment cannot explain behavior, I am not saying it should be ignored, but only that *by itself* it cannot account for human action. I would say that all rational men behave *with respect to* (defined broadly) their environment (if they did not they would be psychotic); but this is not to assert environmental determinism. I am not against measuring the environment, but insofar as one does only that, one is not within the province of psychology *per se,* but rather within the provinces of physics and engineering.

Introspection is not the province of faith or religion. Introspection can and should be objective and scientific. I consider it the basic method of scientific psychology.

Okay, so what are the implications for a manager? Am I saying a manager should be a psychotherapist? No. A manager is not a psychologist and shouldn't be. Should we offer incentives to employees? Certainly. What I'm saying is, the offering of incentives such as money, goal-setting and participation are precisely that; they are incentives, they are not causes. That is why they don't always work, and to know when they will work we have to have some idea about the employees' values, their perceptions of the situation, whether they (as Pat Smith has reiterated many times) trust management — in other words, what cognitive processing they are doing. If we don't know this, we really can't come up with effective policies. The whole point, for instance, of the survey feedback technique is to get some idea of what the employees are thinking so that we can design policies that will at least motivate most of the people. Dr. Hamner claims that we can separate changing the job situation from changing the employee's mind. Such a dichotomy is illusory. If changing the job situation does not change the employee's mind (e.g., goals, knowledge, expectations), then the job changes will not work.

The difference between the behaviorist and the cognitive psychologist is that the behaviorist tries to change employees' minds but denies that he is doing so, while the cognitive psychologist tries to change minds and admits it. I will leave it to the audience to judge which of these procedures is the more ethical.

Clay Hamner: I would like to summarize by listing what I believe to be the areas of agreement and disagreement between us:

1. Professor Locke and I seem to agree that all theories of motivation include cognitive components and that a person's "mind" is an important determinant of behavior. Responsible reinforcement theorists do not dispute this position.

2. Professor Locke seems to disagree with my contentions that:

    a. Cognitions are outcomes of behavior and not causes of behavior.

    b. Cognitions are not sufficient predictors of behavior.

    c. Managers do not and should not try to control directly the cognitive elements of motivation.

    d. Organizational behavior models of motivation should describe the process of how to motivate others and not how to gain self-insight.

    e. Both cognitive and reinforcement theorists have been guilty of shoddy research which keeps us from discovering the truth we both claim to possess or seek.

I think it's time, Ed, that we bury the hatchet. We have really been discussing questions that can be answered empirically if we choose to do so as scientific adversaries. It is time for us to quit talking about rival hypotheses and start testing them.

REFERENCES* (Locke)

Brewer, W.F. There is no convincing evidence for operant or classical conditioning in adult humans, in W. Weimer and D. Palermo (Eds.): *Cognition and the Symbolic Process.* Hillsdale, N.J.: L. Eribaum, 1974.

Deci, E. L. *Intrinsic Motivation.* New York: Plenum Publishing, 1975.

Dulany, D.E., Jr. Awareness, rules and propositional control: a confrontation with S-R behavior theory, in D. Horton and T. Dixon (Eds.): *Verbal Behavior and General Behavior Theory.* Englewood cliffs, N.J.: Prentice-Hall, 1968.

Herrnstein, R.J. Doing what comes naturally: a reply to Professor Skinner. *American Psychologist, 1977, 32,* 1013-1016.

Locke, E.A. The contradiction of epiphenomenalism. *British Journal of Psychology, 1966, 57,* 203-204.

Locke, E. A. Reply to Eysenck et al. *Bulletin of the British Psychological Society, 1969, 22,* 162.

Locke, E. A. Critical analysis of the concept of causality in behavioristic psychology. *Psychological Reports,* 1972, *31,* 175-197.

Locke, E.A., Cartledge, N. and Koeppel, J. Motivational effects of knowledge of results: a goal setting phenomenon? *Psychological Bulletin,* 1968, *70,* 474-485.

Mahoney, M.J. *Cognition and Behavior Modification.* Cambridge: Ballinger, 1974.

Rand, A. *The Virtue of Selfishness.* New York: Signet, 1964.

Skinner, B.F. *Science and Human Behavior.* New York: Free Press, 1953.

Yochelson, S. and Samenow, S. E. *The Criminal Personality* (2 vols.). New York: J. Aronson, 1976/1977.

RECOMMENDED READINGS (Locke)

I. Philosophical Criticisms of Behaviorism

Blanshard, B. Behaviorism and thought, in *The Nature of Thought,* Vol. I. New York: Humanities Press, 1964.
Proves that thought is a conscious process which cannot be identified with any purely physical phenomena.

Chomsky; N. Review of B. F. Skinner's *Verbal Behavior,* in *Language,* 1959, *35,* 26-58.
Documents the unscientific nature of Skinner's treatment of human thought.

Hamlyn, D.W. Conditioning and behavior, in R. Borger and F. Cioffi (Eds.): *Explanation in the Behavioural Sciences.* Cambridge: Cambridge University Press, 1970.
Analyzes the epistemological confusions involved in the concept of "conditioning" as used by behaviorists.

Koestler, A. The poverty of psychology, in *The Ghost in the Machine.* New York: Macmillan Publishing Co., 1967.
Discusses the error of viewing human action as essentially similar to animal behavior.

Locke, E. A. Purpose without consciousness: a contradiction. *Psychological Reports,* 1969, *25,* 991-1009.
Shows why "purpose," and related psychological concepts, cannot be understood without reference to consciousness.

Locke, E.A. Critical analysis of the concept of causality in behavioristic psychology. *Psychological Reports,* 1972, *31,* 175-197.
Analyzes and refutes the concept of causality on which behaviorism is based.

Price, H.H. Some objections to behaviorism, in S. Hook (Ed.): *Dimensions of Mind.* New York: Collier, 1961.
Defends the validity and importance of introspection.

Rand, A. The stimulus and the response. *The Ayn Rand Letter,* 1972, *1,* Nos. 8-11.
Exposes the contradictions in and political dangers of Skinner's attack on freedom and dignity.

II. Behaviorism in Practice

Braginsky, I. and Braginsky, D. Psychotherapy, in *Mainstream Psychology.* New York: Holt, Rinehart and Winston, 1974.
Gives examples of the dictatorial mentality of many behaviorists and shows how in practice they are not at all opposed to the use of forcible punishment of "dissenters."

Brewer, W.F. There is no convincing evidence for operant or classical conditioning in adult humans, in W. Weimer and D. Palermo (Eds.): *Cognition and the Symbolic Processes*. Hillsdale, N.J.: L. Erlbaum, 1974.
Demonstrates that there is no actual evidence for the existence of "conditioning" (learning without awareness) in adult humans.

Locke, E.A. Is "behavior therapy" behavioristic (an analysis of Wolpe's psychotherapeutic methods)? *Psychological Bulletin*, 1971, *76*, 318-327.
Demonstrates why Wolpe's "behavior therapy" is contradictory to the theory of behaviorism.

Locke, E. A. The myths of behavior mod in organizations. *Academy of Management Review*, 1977, *2*, 543-553.
Shows that so-called "behavior modification" techniques used to change employee behavior are neither new nor based on behavioristic principles.

Russell, E. W. The power of behavior control: a critique of behavior modification methods. *Journal of Clinical Psychology*, Monograph Supplement #43, 1974.
Argues and demonstrates by reference to numerous studies that the alleged power of behavior modification techniques to control human behavior is grossly exaggerated.

III. Alternatives to Behaviorism

Arnold, M. Phenomenological analysis of emotion, in *Emotion and Personality*, Vol. I. New York: Columbia University Press, 1960.
Presents a rational nonmaterialistic theory of emotions.

Blumenthal, A. The base of Objectivist psychotherapy. *The Objectivist*, 1969, *8*(6) 6-10; (7) 4-9.
Identifies the basic premises of a rational, scientifically based approach to psychotherapy.

Janis, I. Psychodynamic aspects of stress tolerance, in S. Klausner (Ed.): *The Quest for Self-control*. New York: Free Press, 1965.
Demonstrates the importance of the cognitive element in coping with stress, and shows the deleterious consequences of failing to perform the "work of worrying."

Rand, A. Concepts of consciousness, in *Introduction to Objectivist Epistemology*. New York: The Objectivist Inc., 1967.
Identifies the objective basis for the formulation of concepts referring to states and actions of consciousness.

Sperry, R. A modified concept of consciousness, *and* An objective approach to subjective experience: further explanation of an hypothesis, *Psychological Review*, 1969, *76*, 532-536, *and* 1970, *77*, 585-590.
Offers intriguing hypotheses about the nature of the mind-brain relationship while avoiding the fallacies of monism and Cartesian dualism.

White, R. W. Motivation reconsidered: the concept of competence. *Psychological Review*, 1959, *66*, 297-333.
Exposes the fallacies of behavioristic drive-reduction and psychoanalytic tension-reduction theories of motivation and offers an alternative based on the concept of competence.

Yochelson, S. and Samenow, S. E. *The Criminal Personality*, (2 vols.). New York: J. Aronson, 1976/1977.
Details the authors' discoveries regarding the thinking errors that make up and cause the criminal personality and methods they used to change criminal thinking patterns and criminal behavior.

*Compiled with the help of Dr. Harry Binswanger, Dept. of Philosophy, Hunter College. I am also grateful to Dr. Binswanger for his helpful suggestions regarding the text of the debate.

REFERENCES AND RECOMMENDED READINGS   (Hamner)

Bandura, A. *Social Learning Theory*. Englewood Cliffs, N.J.: Prentice-Hall, 1977.

Bandura, A. *Principles of Behavior Modification*. Holt, Rinehart and Winston, New York, 1969.

Bem, D.J. Self-perception: an alternative interpretation of cognitive dissonance phenomena. *Psychological Review*, 1967, *74*, 183-200.

de Charms, R. *Personal Causation: The Internal Affective Determinants of Behavior*. New York: Academic Press, 1968.

Glaser, R. (Ed.) *The Nature of Reinforcement*. New York: Academic Press, 1971.

Hamner, W. C. Reinforcement theory and contingency management, in H. L. Tosi and W. Clay Hamner (Eds.): *Management and Organizational Behavior*, Chicago: St. Clair Press, 1974.

Hamner, W. C. Management and the study of organizational behavior, in D.W. Organ (Ed.): *The Applied Psychology of Work*. Dallas: Business Publication, Inc. 1978, 7-11.

Hamner, W. C. and Foster, L. W. The effect of intrinsic and extrinsic reinforcement on performance. *Organizational Behavior and Human Performance*, 1975, *14*, 362-398.

Hamner, W. C. and Hamner, E. P. Behavior modification and the bottom line. *Organizational Dynamics*, Spring, 1976, 3-21.

Hamner, W. C. and Organ, D. W. *Organizational Behavior: An Applied Psychological Approach*. Dallas: Business Publication Inc., 1978, especially Chapters 7, 11 and 12.

Hamner, W. C. Mainstone, L. and Ross, J. Combining individual difference, environmental and cognitive variables for exploring worker motivation. Unpublished manuscript, Boston University, 1976.

Hamner, W. C., Ross, J. and Staw, B. Motivation in organizations: the need for a new direction, in D.W. Organ (Ed.): *The Applied Psychology of Work Behavior*, Dallas: Business Publication, Inc., 1978, 224-249.

Hilgrad, E. R. and Bower, G. H. *Theories of Learning,* Fourth Edition. Englewood Cliffs, N.J.: Prentice-Hall, 1975.

Jennings, E. E. *The Mobile Manager.* New York: McGraw-Hill, 1971. Jones, E. E., Kanouse, D. E., Kelley, H. H., Nisbett, R. E., Valins, S. and Weiner, B. *Attribution: Perceiving the Causes of Behavior*. Morristown, N.J.; General Learning Press, 1971.

Kiesler, C. A., Collins, B. E. and Miller, N. *Attitude Change*. New York: John Wiley, 1969.

Kim, J. and Hamner, W. C. The effect of goal setting, feedback and praise on productivity and satisfaction in an organizational setting. *Journal of Applied Psychology*, 1976, *61*, 48-57.

McTeer, W. The scope of motivation. Monterey, Ca.: Brooks/Cole, 1972.

Skinner, B. F. *Contingencies of Reinforcement*. New York: Appleton-Century Crofts, 1969.

Skinner, B. F. *Beyond Freedom and Dignity*. New York: Alfred A. Knopf, 1971.

Staats, A. W. and Staats, C. K. *Complex Human Behavior*. New York: Holt, Rinehart and Winston, 1963.

Valle, F. P. *Motivation: Theories and Issues*. Monterey, Ca.: Brooks/Cole, 1975.

Watson, J. B. *Behaviorism*. New York: Norton, 1924.

Weiner, B. *Theories of Motivation*. Chicago: Markham Publishing Co., 1972.

Zimbardo, P. G. (Ed.). *The Cognitive Control of Motivation*. Glenview, Ill.: Scott, Foresman and Co., 1969a.

Zimbardo, P. G. The human choice: individuation, reason, and order versus deindividuation, impulse, and chaos, in *Nebraska Symposium on Motivation*. Lincoln, Neb.: University of Nebraska, 1969b, 237-309.

Chapter 4

ORGANIZATIONAL BEHAVIOR MODIFICATION

INTRODUCTION

The following debate between Fred Luthans (rhymes with Klingons) and Patricia Cain Smith (rhymes with with) takes a very different tack than the last debate, but you will see some familiar issues. This debate involves application rather than theory: how to diagnose and treat organizational problems. Organizational Behavior Modification, a phrase coined by Luthans and his colleagues, describes a technique, a procedure, rather than a theoretical premise. However, as Pat Smith will argue, this technique rests on some interesting assumptions about science and the practice of management. Watch for them!

After her opening remarks, Pat will seem to digress by offering a broader interpretation of the resolution and of organizational diagnosis than Fred has used. You will, in the bargain, get a good bit of advice on troubleshooting in organizations. There will be many examples to aid you in understanding the real world and real problems of managing. Fred will call Pat's broadened interpretation (he calls it "straying") to our attention in his rebuttal. Yet, whatever the merits of his position, the presentations of these two debators provide a graphic demonstration of difference in style. In a way, their presentations symbolize the differing approaches that characterize cognitive and behavioristic psychology. Straying away, as Fred puts it, it not uncommonly charged by behaviorists when they evaluate the efforts of cognitive psychologists.

While we are on the subject of differences, take careful note of the *domain* that each of these debators is mapping. It will help you to answer the study questions posed in Chapter 2.

Finally, there would seem to be no coincidence in the debators' simultaneous use of "box" imagery. Pat refers to a telephone box, Fred to a Skinner Box. While these uses of the word have quite different meanings, the image is central to the cognitive-behavioristic distinction.

Black box is a metaphor often used to describe the human brain (or soul, or mind). Psychologically, the behaviorists characterize the human mind as unknown, and unknowable, territory. Cognitive psychologists acknowledge the difficulties inherent in gaining access to this black box but insist that the understanding of human behavior, beliefs and values depends on such access. Self-report data are the dominant mode of access. Physiologists, unrepresented in these debates, may ultimately provide means of access that are less subject to perceptual and social distortion than self-report data. Physiology, biology and chemistry are likely to play important roles in resolving issues that now divide behaviorists and cognitive psychologists, as Bill Scott will note in Chapter 6, but for the present, we must work with available data and theory in solving the practical problems of managers and organizations. Let us hand the microphone to a lively pair of debators.

FRED LUTHANS

Fred Luthans teaches and does research in management and organizational behavior at the University of Nebraska. He received his Ph.D. at the University of Iowa and currently holds the National Bank of Commerce Chair of Business Administration at Nebraska.

The author of over a dozen books and fifty articles, Dr. Luthans had the honor of having one of his books, *Organizational Behavior Modification*, named by the American Society of Personnel Administration as the major contribution to human resource management for 1975. It is in this area of the operant approach to human resource management and the General Contingency Theory of Management that Professor Luthans does his basic research and is best known. His O.B. Mod. model is widely

"Resolved: "Functional analysis" is the best technique for diagnostic evaluation of organizational behavior.

Barbara Karmel: Our speakers on this resolution are Fred Luthans for the affirmative and Patricia Cain Smith for the negative.

Fred Luthans: Steve Kerr has suggested that this debate may be our own version of *the Gong Show,* and I have this uneasy feeling that I may be the first one gonged off the stage. Anyway, I would like to begin my affirmative statement with a precise definition of the terms of this resolution. I am not quite sure of its significance, but the key term of our resolution, "functional analysis," is the only one in any of the resolutions that has quotes around it. I conclude from this that while we are all comfortable with such terms as motivation and leadership, we are not quite sure about a behavioristic technique called functional analysis. I think it is critical to our debate to clarify at the beginning exactly what is meant by functional analysis.

My use of functional analysis stems from B.F.Skinner's (1953, p. 35) definition of the term as the analysis of "the external variables of which behavior is a function." The purpose of Skinnerian functional analysis is to predict and control behavior. Grounded in operant learning theory, the technique takes *behavior* as the dependent variable and the *external environment* as independent, causal variables. The word "functional" is borrowed from mathematics and simply means that if one variable changes, then the other variable changes also, or changes in the environment will produce changes in behavior. In summary, based on operant learning theory, behavior is a function of the environment, and functional analysis is a technique for systematically analyzing this relationship for the purpose of predicting and controlling behavior.

With the formal definition serving as a point of departure, functional analysis can be presented operationally in terms of the A (antecedent)–B (behavior)–C (consequence) contingency. The term "contingency" is used by modern behaviorists to identify the relationship between human behavior and its environment. In contrast to the overly simplistic, almost mechanistic, S–R (stimulus–response) contingency, the A–B–C contingency considers both antecedents and consequences as environmental determinants of behavior. The antecedents serve to cue the behavior or set the occasion for a behavior to be emitted. Thus, antecedents can control behavior (usually called stimulus control). For example, if the yellow light on the traffic signal appears when you are approaching a busy intersection, this serves as the occasion or the cue for you to emit certain behaviors. What behavior is emitted will depend on what consequences were forthcoming in the presence of this cue. In the past, if you stepped on the accelerator when the yellow light appeared and the consequence was saving yourself a lot of time and there were no problems, then the next time you see the yellow light you will tend to step on the accelerator again (i.e., you are under stimulus control). On the other hand, suppose that you have the consequence of having an accident or being arrested by stepping on the accelerator in the presence of the yellow light. After the latter experience you would tend to hit the brake when the signal turned yellow. In both cases the antecedent cue (the yellow light) emitted behaviors but, importantly, this cue did not *cause* the behaviors to occur. The antecedent only serves to cue the behavior; the behavior still depends on its consequences. Thus, antecedent cues are important to the prediction and control of behavior, but of even more importance are the contingent consequences. In functional analysis both antecedents and consequences are systematically identified and examined. Before going into this approach further, an example from human resource management may be helpful.

Suppose the manager of the teller department in a large bank was having trouble with one of her tellers being rude to customers. Counseling this employee had no results, so the manager decided to do a functional analysis of the rude behavior. She carefully observed that during rush hours (the antecedent) this teller was very rude to customers (the behavioral event). This behavior resulted in getting rid of disgruntled customers quickly and causing them to look for other tellers in subsequent trips to the bank (the consequence). In short, the functional analysis revealed that the rush hours cued or set the occasion for the rude behavior to be emitted. Getting rid of customers and not having them return was maintaining and strengthening the rude behavior. This functional analysis seems vital to the diagnostic evaluation of the teller's behavior.

By now we hopefully have a clear understanding of what is meant by functional analysis. However, I do not want to quit my definitional tactics quite yet. I think that the other part of our resolution which says what the functional analysis technique is aimed at — "the diagnostic evaluation of organizational behavior" — also deserves special attention. Taking one word at a time, the commonly accepted meaning of (1) "diagnostic" is to recognize and identify by examination and *observation;* (2) "evaluation" is a systematic appraisal; and (3) "organizational behavior" is one or more *observable* events, something the organizational participant *does* rather than something that is done to the participant or something that goes on inside the participant's head. Now, I suppose one could argue the fine points of what I have just said, but I really think we can all pretty much agree that my definitions capture the essence of the meaning of our resolution. If you agree with me, then I have gone a long way in supporting the affirmative position simply by defining the terms.

If the terms are understood, there seems little doubt that functional analysis is the best technique for diagnostic evaluation of organizational behavior. The resolution is aimed at observable behaviors, not unobservable inner states such as needs or attitudes, or metaphors such as organizational health or climate. Why should we opt for observables rather than inner states? Take popular hypothetical constructs such as motivation or leadership. I think we sometimes forget that these constructs do not exist in empirical reality; they are not directly observable or measurable. I challenge you to show me a leadership or a motivation. All you can point to are behaviors that you then *attribute* to certain motivational or leadership processes.

Another example will help illustrate what I am trying to get at here. Suppose you observe an employee walking briskly into the company cafeteria. Why is he behaving this way? Most people would attribute this behavior to the hunger motive. In other words, an unobservable, hypothetical construct labeled "hunger motivation" is used to explain this behavior. When this inference is used, prediction and control of the behavior are ignored and the explanation is very imprecise. Is hunger really causing the observed behavior, or is it sex (he wants to get a date with the cashier) or affiliation (he wants to meet with his friends who congregate at the cafeteria) or power (he wants to be seen eating with the boss) or any of a multitude of other possibilities? And how are these attributes determined and measured? Most often by standardized questionnaires that have predetermined response sets and come up with pooled estimates and perceptions that generally have little or no relationship to actual behaviors or outcomes. (For example, a study by Azrin et al. (1961) found that the questionnaire responses of their subjects were independent of the behavior being studied.) However, it must be remembered that the point in this discussion is *not* whether complex inner causes exist or dont't exist. In light of our resolution, the question to be answered is whether this internal approach (analysis of inner states), with its accompanying indirect questionnaire measurement techniques, is as effective as an external approach (observable behavior) that examines environmental contingencies through the direct technique of functional analysis. Obviously, for the purpose of diagnostic evaluation of organizational behavior, I am arguing that analyzing observable environmental contingencies is a better method than searching for unobservable inner causes through imprecise measurement techniques.

The argument in favor of functional analysis becomes even stronger if we can agree that prediction and control are desirable goals to attain with our techniques. As was discussed earlier in the example of the traffic signal, both the antecedents and the consequences play a vital role in prediction and control. By working with the antecedent side of functional analysis, one can determine if the behavior in question is under stimulus control. Using a terminology based on the principles derived from discrimination learning, we can use SD to represent that stimulus in whose presence a behavior is reinforced and S^Δ to represent that stimulus in whose presence there is no reinforcement. Once these SD/S^Δ 's are identified through functional analysis, we can predict behavior by observing the presence of SD/S^Δ and can control the behavior by intervening with the appropriate SD/S^Δ. For example, the functional analysis of the person's behavior of walking into the cafeteria may reveal that certain times of the day serve as an SD for the behavior to be emitted. By identifying such SD's and S^Δ 's through functional analysis, this behavior and other more complex organizational behaviors can be predicted and possibly controlled.

The consequence side of functional analysis is even more critical to the goals of prediction and control than are the antecedents. Based on Thorndike's widely accepted Law of Effect, one of the true functional laws in the behavioral sciences, we know that behavior followed by positive consequences (positive reinforcers) will strengthen and increase in frequency; behavior followed by negative consequences (punishers) will weaken and decrease in frequency; and behavior followed by neutral or no consequences (extinction) will tend to weaken and decrease in frequency. This law, of course, allows one to predict and control behaviors. Using the same earlier example, if our functional analysis indicates that the person received a positive consequence for going into the cafeteria, we can be confident in our prediction that he will go back again. By the same token, if we find that he received a negative or no consequence, then we can be confident in our prediction that the frequency of going into the cafeteria will decrease. We can also control his behavior by contingently applying positive (negative) consequences to increase (decrease) his behavior.

To anticipate my opponent's counterarguments, let me quickly add the following. I recognize, all too well, that the two biggest complaints with my position are: (1) Okay, I agree with the Law of Effect, but for prediction and control, how do you know what is a positive or negative consequence? and (2) The Law of Effect may be true, but, except for cats in a puzzle box or rats in a Skinner Box, the contingencies for organizational behavior are too complex and difficult to identify, and thus prediction and control become virtually impossible. In answer to the first question, let me respond that a positive consequence is defined simply as anything which leads to an increase in behavioral frequency, and a negative consequence is anything which leads to a decrease in behavioral frequency. Before you laugh too loud or accuse me of using circular definitions, let me point out that I am still using an *operational* definition, and past experience gives us a pretty good indication of what is positive and what negative for people in organizations. Even though the definition is admittedly circular, by *observing* what impact a consequence has had on subsequent behavior, we can operationally determine if the consequence was positive or negative. Furthermore, we have sufficient evidence from research and experience that indicates, at least for practical purposes, that organizational participants regard recognition/attention and feedback as positive consequences. Notice I did not say something like praise. There are individual differences in reactions to praise, some of which may not be positive. The same could be said of money, time off and many other possible rewards. One way of getting around this problem is simply to ask the person what a desirable or undesirable consequence is, or to examine systematically the person's reinforcement history. To summarize, I do admit that an a priori designation of a particular consequence as being positive or negative is a legitimate concern. By observing the impact of the consequence using certain predictable consequences, such as attention/recognition and feedback, and asking/analyzing reinforcement histories, one can overcome this problem. In any event, this potential problem certainly does not seem severe enough to dismiss functional analysis as an effective method of predicting and controlling the behavior of individuals in organizations.

The second problem (contingencies are too complex) is admittedly more difficult to counter than the first. There is little question that, as one critic brilliantly observed, modern organizations are not the same as Skinner Boxes. It is obviously much more difficult to identify and analyze the contingencies of human behavior in complex organizations than infrahuman behavior under highly controlled laboratory conditions. For example, suppose we want to predict and control the bank teller's rude behavior mentioned earlier. The functional analysis revealed that time was an antecedent and getting rid of customers was a consequence. For this, and many other organizational behaviors, the antecedent conditions may be difficult to change, i.e., we cannot change time or an employee's home life or, in some cases, the technological processes of the job. However, this admission that some factors are uncontrollable does not imply that antecedents are off limits in predicting and controlling organizational behaviors. Prompting, shaping and modeling strategies can be used effectively on most types of employee behaviors. In prompting, a request, question, command or suggestion is used to cue the appropriate behavior which is then reinforced. Shaping, of course, has tremendous potential for changing employee behavior. By reinforcing successive approximations, the employer can encourage the employee gradually to attain the targeted behavior. Under a shaping strategy, any improvement is reinforced. Modeling also holds great promise as a behavioral change strategy. The person learns by observation and imitation, rather than by a number of trials. Especially valuable in the training process, modeling can be used to introduce complex, unfamiliar behaviors to employees.

The area of organization development (OD) provides an example of how the understanding and analysis of antecedents can be applied. Most of the OD strategies (e.g., job enrichment, conflict resolution or team building) can be employed to set the occasion and cue appropriate productive behaviors. But it must be remembered that antecedents only become an SD and control behavior to the extent that reinforcing consequences follow the behavior that has been emitted. This last point may help to explain why many OD programs are only effective in the short run. They carefully structure the organizational environment (e.g., mechanisms for conflict reduction or an enriched task design) that set the occasion for desirable employee behaviors to be emitted, but then fail to provide the contingent reward systems to reinforce these behaviors. With no reinforcement, the OD program loses its stimulus control power over productive employee behaviors and becomes ineffective.

Besides the important role that antecedents can and do play in predicting and controlling organizational behavior, as has been emphasized throughout the discussion, consequences are even more important. Let's use the previous example of the bank teller's rude behavior to demonstrate the role of contingent consequences. To alter this rude behavior we have to change the consequence. Remember, this behavior would not be occurring unless it were being reinforced. Suppose the manager, relying on the Law of Effect, decides that to decrease this rude behavior she has to administer a negative consequence. She decides the best way to do this is to chew the teller out the next time she observes her rude behavior. After doing this, however, the manager observes that the rude behavior actually increases in frequency. Her intervention strategy turns out to have an effect opposite to that intended. The critic would jump on this result and say, "Where is your prediction and control now?" The answer, of course, is that one of two things happened. First, the manager did not apply a negative consequence. The observable data suggest that the chewing out was actually a positive consequence for this employee. What might have happened was that the chewing out was seen as attention from the manager, a desirable consequence. As was stated earlier, we have found attention very reinforcing for most employees, even negative attention. In fact, any attempt to control human behavior using negative consequences may produce many types of unpredictable and undesirable side effects. A second explanation, and the one that is more directly related to the issue of environmental complexity, is that getting chewed out was not the *contingent* consequence for the rude behavior. In complex environments such as this bank, there are many competing contingencies for employee behavior. In this case, some obvious consequences of the rude behavior, in addition to the manager's wrath, are getting rid of customers, co-workers smiling and even congratulating the teller for her rude behavior, co-workers envying her "guts" and many other possibilities.

Okay, if we acknowledge the complexities of organizational environment, where does this leave us in terms of using functional analysis to reach the goals of prediction and control of organizational behavior? In the first place, the manager of the teller department, as well as human resource managers in general, would be more effective if she concentrated on accelerating desirable employee behaviors rather than attempting to decelerate undersirable behaviors. The manager in the example would have more success if she contingently rewarded the teller's courteous behavior with attention/recognition and feedback. This type of positive control is much more effective in changing organizational behaviors. Unfortunately, unless human resource managers make a concerted effort to take the positive approach, they tend to be ineffective because of their reliance on negative control. Too often when managers observe desirable employee behaviors, i.e., those that contribute to goals, they either say to themselves, "Well, it's about time" and provide no consequence (which, of course, leads to extinction of the behavior), or they falsely assume, "Finally, she is doing what she is getting paid to do." Managers must realize that most wages (exceptions would be sales commissions and some, but not most, incentive systems) are administered on such a noncontingent basis that they have nothing to do with reinforcing day-to-day job behaviors. By the same token, many managers are unwittingly reinforcing inappropriate behaviors. For example, the manager who makes it a practice periodically to bring his group together and indiscriminantly tell them all they are doing a "good job" may be ineffective. By this noncontingent praise he is rewarding those who deserve it as well as those who do not deserve it in terms of improved performance and goal attainment.

I am not trying to minimize the difficulty of contingency analysis and management in a complex setting such as that found in modern organizations. What I am saying is that this problem is not insurmountable. We can overcome much of this problem through a systematic approach to organizational behavior modification (see Luthans and Kreitner, 1975). I am asking that the baby not be thrown out with the bathwater. Organizational behavior *is* a function of the antecedent and consequent environment, and functional analysis *is* the best technique for the diagnostic evaluation of organizational behavior.

To summarize my position on the resolution, I would like to emphasize the following points. When the terms of our resolution are defined, it becomes very clear that we should aim our discussion at observable behaviors and not at unobservable inner states, such as feelings, needs and values, or metaphors such as organizational health or climate. I do not think we should lose sight of the importance of a behavioral focus in this debate, or in the field of organizational behavior for that matter. I think that when we treat hypothetical constructs or metaphors as ends in themselves, we are led up too many blind alleys in our search for the goals of understanding, prediction and control. If we can accept that the focus should be on behavior, then it is only a matter of determining the best way to make a diagnostic evaluation of it. Following operant learning theory, I have argued that behavior is largely a function of the environment. This, of course, does not suggest that inner states do not exist, a fact Skinner himself recognizes in discussing covert operants that help to explain human behavior. What I do suggest is that we recognize the important role that the environment plays in organizational behavior. It follows that, by systematic analysis of observable antecedents and contingent conse-

PATRICIA CAIN SMITH

Patricia Cain Smith received a Ph.D. in Industrial Psychology from Cornell University and is presently Professor of Psychology at Bowling Green and supervisor of Cain-Smith Associates, industrial consultants.

Dr. Smith is the author or coauthor of more than a hundred publications. Her chief consulting and research interests are the areas of organizational diagnosis, industrial motivation and satisfaction, interrelations of health, family and community, and life and job satisfaction, as well as employee selection, interviewing, performance evaluation and employee development. She is co-author of two books: *Principles of Industrial Psychology* and *The Measurement of Satisfaction in Work & Retirement.*

Dr. Smith is consulting editor for *Organizational Behavior and Human Performance* and *Perceptual and Motor Skills* and has served on the Council of the American Psychological Association.

quences through the technique called functional analysis, we can best accomplish the charge of our resolution, which is to find the best way to make a diagnostic evaluation of organizational behavior.

Pat Smith: In preparing material for this debate we were asked to take an extreme position in order to make our differences very clear. I think, however, that my honorable opponent was a sucker to take the extreme position he did, but I might as well enjoy it.

Obviously, there is no one best technique for diagnosing behavior in all organizations or situations, although there is a best goal or plan of approach. We need to employ all available tools, whether they are called subjective or objective, for solving the problems involved in the diagnosis of behavior in organizations. We cannot ignore the individual's thoughts, feelings and values. These determine, govern and direct organizational performance and behavior.

Maybe the analogy of a trouble-shooter for the telephone company will clarify the process required for diagnosis and repair of a machine (or an organization) that isn't working properly. We do not send a person out on a repair job who knows only how to dial a phone, who understands only that when one sees a telephone (antecedent), one can insert a finger sequentially into each of a series of holes on a dial. The expert rotates the dial (behavior) and experiences a ringing sound (consequence). If something goes wrong with the mechanism, this person has no choice but to continue mindlessly repeating the behavior that has been reinforced in the past (until, of course, he or she exhibits emotional behavior and takes an axe to the phone). He has no choice because he cannot invoke understanding to formulate new plans or intentions to perform alternative behaviors. As a slave to what has been reinforced in the past, he is destined to continue the same behavior until it becomes extinguished. There is no provision in his system for changing his behavior voluntarily, just as there is no provision for innovation in traditional reinforcement theory.

If it were my telephone company, I would want the troubleshooter to understand the "works" (the inner state) of the machine. I would want someone who could and would remove the exterior case, examine the mechanism, make a sensible guess (hypothesis) about what is wrong, check to see if a change based on that guess improves performance, and if necessary try other possibilities until the apparatus works normally. The A–B–C-contingency is simply not enough. It is not the whole alphabet. It is not even the shrewdest way to begin to search for the most frequently used letters in the alphabet. In other words, to diagnose what is wrong and repair it, we need to get inside the head of the human being or beneath the surface of observable behavior in an organization.

What do we mean by diagnosis? My large dictionary (Random House, 1973) gives five definitions, all of which imply or specify "understanding." Two of them seem to apply particularly to the kind of diagnosis we are talking about here:

. . . the process of determining by examination the nature and circumstances of a diseased condition . . . [and] a determining or analysis of the cause or nature of a problem or situation.

Determining nature, circumstances and causes implies something more than the simple counting of the frequency with which one event follows another. In giving it the name "functional analysis," Fred doesn't make it more effective in solving behavioral problems. Problem-solving — the essence of diagnosis, as any physician will tell you — involves hypotheses about *causes*. Understanding, rather than trial and error, marks the skilled diagnostician.

(Patients become *im*patient if first the appendix, then the gallbladder, then the tonsils are removed because the physician is trying various treatments to see what works, to find his reinforcer).

Diagnosis is complex. There are usually many factors which interact and form a pattern in determining what each individual does, and hence, the effectiveness of the organization. Physical and social situations differ from organization to organization; the backgrounds, abilities and aspirations of the employees differ even more widely; the characteristics of communities, which affect the way individuals evaluate their own working situations, also vary. We could, I suppose, start from scratch in each new plant or organization and busily count behaviors to find out what reinforcers there are, but that approach certainly seems grossly inefficient. If we can instead formulate general laws which specify how these factors interact, we can generalize across situations and people. We will be able simply to measure the required variables (subjective and objective), plug the values into a set of complex equations, and predict, without trial and error, how a particular group of people will respond to a particular managerial act. Knowing these laws means that, in a scientific sense, we understand causes.

One of the variables that links managerial action to subsequent behavior is intention. Intention has repeatedly proved to be the best single predictor of actual subsequent behavior and to be essential to prediction of response to intended incentives. (For prediction of productivity, see the numerous goal-setting studies: Latham and Yukl, 1975a, b, 1976; Latham, Mitchell and Dossett, 1978; Locke, 1968. For prediction of quitting or turnover, see Kraut, 1975; LaRocco, Pugh and Gunderson, 1977. For an understanding of the explanatory use of intention, see Ryan, 1970 — a difficult but convincing exposition.)

Interviews with people leaving their jobs, and with dissatisfied people who are nevertheless not leaving, make it clear that people behave contrary to their intentions usually for reasons beyond their control, such as their family situations, the job market and economic limitations. These factors are also beyond the control of management. They seem, at this stage, to set an upper limit to the accuracy of any prediction of actual behavior. I believe that, at least in some situations, we would get clearer laws and better understanding if we tried to predict, control and understand the relationships between other variables and *intentions* rather than actual behavior with its large unpredictable component.

Observation of the behavior of others is extremely useful. It is, however, quite unreliable unless observers are very carefully trained and limited to observation of very specific actions. Unfortunately, people who have not participated in research on accuracy of observation of behavior have a complacent belief in their own uncanny powers. This belief seems to persist in the face of overwhelming evidence to the contrary. We are all familiar with some version of the testimony demonstration, in which a scene is displayed on a screen or portrayed by actors in a short sequence of actions in front of an audience. Immediately afterwards, the members of the audience report what they "saw", with astonishing and amusing variability among observers (and discrepancy from the facts). These dramatic demonstrations of errors of observation were reported early in this century. Since the results are so consistently appalling, the demonstrations are a favorite to this day with teachers of such subjects as elementary psychology and legal psychology. Studies of the reliability of time-study observations have also shown repeatedly that observers disagree to a distressing extent, but their irrational belief in their accuracy of observation persists (Lifson, 1953).

Observation is frequently inaccurate not only because of random error, but also because the bias of the observer distorts what he or she thinks took place. Studies demonstrating the effects of bias are also very old and continue to the present.

Systematic analysis and training can increase consistency and accuracy of observation. If, moreover, the extensive research on test construction and psychometric scaling is applied, observations can be made much more useful. We can even show that the behaviors we observe are relevant to the goals of the individual and the organization. Sometimes we relate observation to the verbal report of the individual — to prove the validity of the *observation,* incidentally, not vice versa. Psychologists who have their eyes on the profit and loss statement don't want to waste time observing trivial and irrelevant behavior, just because it can be counted. When we look at the broad spectrum of information needed for diagnosis, observation enters primarily in the primitive, intuitive, initial phases of study of the situation and in the last phases, after understanding has been achieved and when we count behaviors to prove how much money we have saved (or made) for the organization.

Even the simplest of behaviors can arise from different causes. Whether a proposed reinforcer will modify a particular behavior depends on its cause. For example, a person may be frequently tardy. Giving a reward (money, approval) whenever he or she arrives on time may be very effective if the tardiness has been caused by taking the last bus rather than the one before it, or if the alarm clock has been set at the last possible minute, or if one more cup of coffee has seemed more important than being at work exactly on time. But if there is only one morning bus or train, or the worker is dependent upon a car pool with no alternative transportation, or if he or she must wait until some other member of the family is picked up by a similarly unreliable car pool, the reward may be not only ineffective but also stressful.

More complex behavior can be caused by several interlocking factors. Let's take the common problem that the people in a given department resist a change in method of doing their work, such as the introduction of a new piece of equipment. We could perform a functional analysis and try to find a consequence which will increase the frequency of use of the new method. We might, sometimes after several unsuccessful trials, find a consequence which does modify behavior.

Alternatively, we could try to find out whether workers feared that some of them would be laid off if, for example, new equipment did their work. Perhaps, on the other hand, they feel that they would lose prestige if their jobs were mechanized or automated. We would find out whether some formal or informal leader had strong beliefs and feelings about the effects of the machine and had led the group to exert pressure against change. We would try to assess whether the employees believed what they had been told about the new method, and whether they trusted their management. We would check to see if the equipment was difficult to operate, was uncomfortable, produced too many defective pieces, required delays in getting the work done or was otherwise undesirable. If facts supported use of the equipment, we would consider the feelings of the workers and try to change those feelings. We would attempt to persuade people that the use of the machine would benefit them, would be in line with their own goals. We would not be frightened by the accusation that we were unscientific or subjective. We would instead feel confident that we were including as many relevant variables as possible, in a meaningful and lawful way, to improve the precision of our predictions. We would not take either a change or a lack of change in frequency of behavior to be evidence of whether we had discovered a potentially effective reinforcer.

It is all too easy to point out the inadequacies of a single simplistic approach like functional analysis. I want, instead, to be constructive. I have my own, much more complex, "best" sequence of steps to improve an organization. Note the use of *sequence,* rather than one single step. We must use many different techniques. We must vary them to suit a particular situation according to information as we obtain it.

There are six principal steps in the overall plan: (1) setting goals and criteria, (2) evaluating the situation, (3) integrating the information, (4) recommending action, (5) evaluating outcomes and (6) reporting results. Each involves many different techniques, only a few of which I will mention here.

The sequence of steps is necessary to insure the relevance of the interventions we undertake to the long-term goals of both the organization and the people in it. It is essential to look at the pattern of events and evidence, rather than to single out isolated forms of behavior for change, as in fuctional analysis. We must not rush in where angels fear to tread, before we know what is, and should be, going on.

ESTABLISH GOALS AND CRITERIA

First, there is the issue of recognizing organizational health or the lack of it. Profitability figures are not enough; an organization may be very sick, on the verge of collapse, and still be showing profits on the profit and loss statement.

Since immediate profits alone are not sufficient, what are to be our criteria for a healthy organization? Until we establish what we are trying to accomplish, we will never know whether or not we have succeeded. We cannot set these criteria from an armchair, as functional analysts imply — "It would be better if workers increased their rate of attendance, because absence is obviously bad" — without determining whether absence is an important organizational problem.

We must clarify the goals of the organization, and of the people in it. What do people at different levels and in different departments think the goals should be? Do they agree with one another? (Frequently, they don't). Individually, what do employees say about their own goals? What do they want and expect from their employers? What do the employers expect in return? Can organizational and individual goals be made compatible? Employees and their immediate supervisors disagree even about the duties involved in the job, and about what the supervisor does. (For example, see Besco and Lawshe, 1959; Zedeck and Baker, 1972.) How, therefore, do we deal with lack of congruence in perceptions of goals and activities?

We consider money-related goals, of course — profits, costs and wages — in most organizations. If profits and cost containment are goals, how much should be considered profitable and economical? How much pay should be considered fair (Zedeck and Smith, 1968)? What levels of such personnel statistics as production, absence, turnover and training time should be considered cost-efficient? Are we supposed to look for immediate profit or for long-term growth? There are many such questions. The whole problem of establishing relevant criteria is complicated (see Smith, 1976).

Are the only goals monetary ones? Both businesses and nonprofit organizations publicly express goals such as service to the community and to society.

In hospitals and welfare agencies, for example, these goals are supposedly predominant. To an increasing extent, however, the business community acknowledges such responsibility and donates employees' time and company facilities toward public service activities. Perhaps business merely believes that good public relations lead to both a better quality of employees and better performance. Company reputation and stability of employment are often explicitly stated as goals.

Since we at first so often find such startling disagreement among people about the goals of the organization, we must bring them together for discussion until they concur to a reasonable degree. Otherwise, we can never know whether we have succeeded in achieving the "actual" goals which should be reached. This "thrashing out" of goals is extremely therapeutic (if painful) in itself. It leads to agreement about what measures of success will be acceptable, to establishing criteria for organizational health.

The first step, then, is to make sure we know where we are trying to go and to determine how we will know when or if we have gotten there. This clarification enables us to start the next step, which involves finding out where the strengths and weaknesses lie, so we can start diagnosis of causes.

EVALUATE THE PRESENT SITUATION

Diagnosis requires evaluation of the way the organization and its members are now functioning in comparison with what we have determined to be desirable.

Where do we stand when we start to achieve these agreed-upon goals? We start by evaluating the present health of our organization and its members. We begin by using the most obvious and easily available diagnostic tools, and we look for the most frequent sources of trouble. For example, we look at available records, reports and written policies; we look around (unreliable as observation may be) and tap the grapevine (possibly even less reliable), all to give us an idea of where to look more carefully and deeply. On the basis of hunches (or more formal hypotheses) which we get from these initial data, we "zero in" on problem areas, using more and more detailed and specialized tools to get information. We choose aids for diagnosis in the order in which we think they will give us the most information most efficiently. These aids are both subjective and objective (see Zedeck and Blood, 1974, pp.90-107; or for a much older source, Ryan and Smith, 1954, pp. 298-301).

The advocates of functional analysis admit that when they are in an actual working situation they freely use people's verbal reports about what rewards they want, so that the "scientists" can determine what reinforcers to use in attempting to change behavior (Luthans and Kreitner, 1975, pp. 91-99). The trouble is that functional analysts consider verbal reports "unscientific" and thus frequently ignore the technical literature which indicates how to ask questions, how to design a study of values or attitudes or, for that matter, how to interview or how to sell.

Let's forget, at least for a moment, the rather useless distinction between subjective reports produced by emitting words, orally or in writing, as contrasted with objective behavior produced by the action of other sets of muscles. Where will we get the greatest amount of useful information most efficiently? Where should we look first?

Records. Much pay dirt is available in the office records, which give us important clues about what is going on. These are particularly desirable sources of ideas, since they are inexpensive and we don't need to disrupt any operations to use them.

One source is attendance reports. Absence data are usually tabulated separately by departments, in either the payroll or personnel office. If a particular department is markedly different from others, we investigate. Could it be dissatisfaction with some aspects of the job which can easily be improved, such as working conditions? (I did work in one plant where the paint sprayers had no exhaust fans, so that workers had to breathe the fine spray of enamel. One man told me that he routinely vomited at the end of every working day. I might not have known about this "behavior" if I had not looked at absence rates). Alternatively, absences could have been the result of lax or unfair supervision. This interpretation can and should be checked. Many other explanations will come to your mind; consider how each could be checked to see if it is plausible.

Another source of information is the distribution of output of workers in each department. (This particular source has been known so long that it has lost novelty and isn't even covered in most recent textbooks. Many young people going into management positions have never even heard of it — perhaps another example of the tendency of behavioral scientists to pursue a novel fad rather than to direct their efforts toward maximal payoff). Briefly, if nothing except individual differences in abilities and drive determined how much each person produced, we would find the output in a department to be distributed according to the familiar bell-shaped curve. The poorer producer would perhaps show one-seventh the output of the best. Note in passing that this scientific prediction comes from an analysis of two inner states — ability and drive.

Of course, there are a number of factors that change the bell-shaped distribution. The very incompetent do, indeed, usually quit, get fired, transfer or even get kicked upstairs. The very good do sometimes get promoted. These procedures diminish the number of people in the two tails of the distribution. But over and above these influences, there are *beliefs* among workers which result in a sharp upper limit to the distribution of output, beyond which almost no one goes.

An output curve with no obvious upper tail, or with a very narrow variation around the mean, is a signal flag to us as investigators and warns us about the reward system in that operating unit. We can pretty well bet that employees are restricting their output according to a code mutually agreed upon or at least enforced by the group. The code punishes the rate-buster who exceeds a specified level of production. The code has developed because employees *believe* that if anyone produces more than a certain amount, some joker from the front office will arrive with a stop watch, declaring that the job has changed since the previous standards or work quotas were established. The time-study person will then retime the job and set new, tighter standards. In plain English, this will mean that the employees will have to do more work for the same pay. It takes exactly one such foolish breach of faith by management to insure that a so-called incentive system becomes ineffective, or even that no one works hard to get promoted. Moreover, the word spreads like a flash fire throughout the company. Management has then lost one crucial ingredient of a healthy system. It is called confidence or *trust*. Unfortunately, the loss of trust and the restriction of output are very evident today, just as they were when they were documented by Mathewson in 1931.

There is an important difference between restriction of output (enforced by codes) and another limitation of production which I call pacing. One can also detect pacing from the records. Even when there is no restriction of output, even when different individuals produce different amounts, we can look at variability for each individual from day to day or week to week. If there is *not* considerable variation, there are several possibilities. One is that the flow of work doesn't permit people to produce at their maxima. If so, job redesign is in order. More likely, workers are pacing their own work. It is normal for each of us to set a goal which we intend to accomplish each day (See Roethlisberger and Dixon, 1939; Smith, 1953). But if we do not raise these goals periodically, it means that we are not *thinking* about getting ahead, not *trying* either to make more money or to get promoted. We *intend* to produce the same amount each day. Too much self-pacing at a fixed rate suggests to the shrewd diagnostician that the lines of promotion are not open, or that the employees *think* or *believe* either that the lines are not open or that promotion leads to nothing worthwhile. We have known about restriction and pacing for a very long time, as you can tell from the dates on the references I have cited.

Rothe (see his 1978 article for the most recent study and a summary) has suggested that we can better assess the effectiveness of an incentive system by examining the consistency of output from week to week. He does not distinguish between restriction and pacing, and feels that low correlations of individuals' outputs from week to week indicate low "incentivation." We should examine these correlations to see if some individuals are setting a consistently high goal for themselves while others are setting consistently low goals, that is, pacing as contrasted with random fluctuations. Pacing does seem to be favored by clear standards, such as those set by time-study analysts in establishing a piece-rate or other incentive program in which pay is related to output. The correlations across time should be informative.

Note that I have deliberately been using a lot of words like *believe, intend, think, try* and *trust*, which refer to processes going on within the person, and which are not directly observable. But functional analysis abhors the mention of such inner states. It avoids dealing with well-known facts, such as: if workers are told they will receive a reward if they reach a certain level of production, and if they accept *(believe)* that statement, production increases immediately, *before* any actual reinforcement has taken place. (I enjoy taking my evidence from the findings of behavior modifiers themselves, such as Feeney, 1973, or McGinnies, 1970). *We* do not use circular reasoning to infer these subjective states from the behavior which follows them, but rather from the antecedent verbal behaviors of the managers and workers.

It is almost impossible to discuss behavior in real life without introducing subjective terms or referring to inner states. For example, in Fred's example of the rude teller, he used "attention" as a possible reinforcer for the undesirable behavior. I'm sure he really meant "perceived attention," a thoroughly subjective state. Despite their pretenses of scientific purity secured by avoiding the use of the subjective, it is quite obvious that modern practitioners of Skinnerian principles rely heavily on subjective reports.

By the way, it is not only Skinnerians who caution that relying solely on questionnaires can lead to studies with little relation to behavior. Studies of self-reports related only to other self-reports can be unrealistic, circular and misleading. Hence, few are undertaken and fewer escape the red pens of editors, non-Skinnerian as well as Skinnerian, and are actually published.

Other figures available from records are useful. Gathering the information is equally unobtrusive and nondisruptive. Turnover, accidents, scrap, grievances, suggestions and transfer requests are examples of other records which may signal areas of organizational sickness or health. We get as much information from situations where things seem to be exceptionally healthy as from those where things are obviously sick. In either case, we follow up to make certain about our suspicions and to plan possible actions.

Company policies. What is the present status of programs for selection, placement, training and promotion of employees if, indeed, there are planned programs? Can they be improved (Guion, 1976; Hinrichs, 1976)? What is the nature of the jobs? How have they been designed? We look at job design from two points of view, not necessarily in conflict. First, are operations efficient? Are working time and effort being wasted on unnecessary activities? Does the work flow smoothly, and does each person feel that what he does is useful? (Much maligned "efficiency experts" can actually build morale, since there is no more negative word one can apply to one's job than "useless." For a clear explication of how to reduce needless effort, see McCormick, 1976). On the other hand, we try to see that jobs are designed so that the person feels that he or she has control over the pace and timing, the method and the quality of the work. This autonomy seems to be at the heart of the job enrichment programs.

The feeling of the individual that he has some control over the situation is clearly a subjective state, one that is frequently reported by workers. But there is evidence even from animal studies that it can serve as a reinforcer of behavior. A carefully trained Skinnerian psychologist, Badia (see, for example, Badia and Culbertson, 1972) has repeatedly shown that rats will press a lever just to receive a warning signal, even when shock is inevitable whatever the rat does. The explanation of the behavior in noncognitive terms becomes very involved. It is more convenient for me, as a scientist, to consider that it is subjectively less unpleasant to know when the shock will come than to remain in suspense. I suppose that we could ignore that feeling and simply report that information acts as a reinforcer.

But how does a scientist get around the fact that in man, also, it is not his actual control of his environment but *belief* in his self-control that effectively changes behavior?

Rumor. Measurement is essential to science, but so also is insight, which is sometimes triggered by very qualitative observations or information from dubiously reliable sources. So, while we are working on the records and examining procedures, we should also be tapping the grapevine. Valuable allies are the switchboard operator, the night watchman, the people who empty the wastebaskets and others outside the front office who move around in the building or are otherwise in the know. It is informative, sometimes, to sit with open ears in the neighborhood bars where employees cash their paychecks. The graffiti on the walls of the washrooms are sometimes as informative as amusing. Of course, we don't believe all we hear and see, but we become alert to variables which we must investigate more carefully.

Standardized measuring instruments. Industrial sociologists have given us reliable tools to assess organizational characteristics such as mechanization, formalization and autonomy (Price, 1972). We use them if we feel that we should probe into the way the organization functions. Industrial psychologists have given us ways of measuring individual characteristics. Interviews may give us a good start, but if we want reliable figures which can be compared across the organization, we will use standardized questionnaires and tests. Routinely, we measure satisfaction with various aspects of the job. [It should be done every six months, and followed up with more intensive study wherever things have changed (Landy and Trumbo, 1976, pp. 355-364; Smith, Kendall and Hulin, 1969).] We measure what people value in their work and try to tailor personnel policies to these values (Wollack, Goodale, Wijting and Smith, 1971).

Observation. We observe people working. We watch their faces as we walk through the plant with the manager. We might even stand around and count frequencies of different kinds of behavior, that is, perform what has recently been renamed functional analysis; but if so, it would be only one part of a systematic investigation of all available cues. We would remember the depressingly poor accuracy of observers' ratings of behavior (Lifson, 1953; Ryan, 1947). Moreover, we would have developed the basis for deciding *which* kinds of behavior to count, because those behaviors *meant* something about individual and organizational goals, not merely because they occurred frequently.

I am reminded of an example of counting frequencies which had many implications for the design of work (Smith and Lem, 1955). We have all experienced the pull to complete a unit of work, to finish a task before taking a break. This pull, called "traction" by Baldamus (1951), should be reflected in spacing of voluntary rest pauses. The pull seems to be greatest toward the end of a task unit. Therefore, based on Baldamus and our subjective experience, we predicted that production workers would work longer between rest pauses when the units were short enought so that the end was in sight throughout, but still long enough so that each formed a meaningful whole. In addition, workers should then take fewer breaks. If workers were restricting output, the change in traction would appear in rest pauses, not (at least at first) in production.

We grabbed the opportunity provided by a fortunate request for help to conduct a field experiment to test these predictions. A small department in a cooperative company showed *no* variance in production from individual to individual, from morning to afternoon, or from day to day. Everyone produced one "tote pan" of 7100 pieces of work per four-hour period. By some miracle of computation by the time-study "experts," all the jobs had received the same time standard, despite considerable apparent variation in the operations involved. All tasks were light and apparently repetitive. The workers were obviously taking very many rest pauses.

We started timing their activities. They were aware of our presence, but after a pre-experimental period of adaptation, they got used to us and returned to their normal activities, including the observer in their jokes and conversation. We counted any period of 30 seconds or longer away from the machine as a voluntary break. After securing a base rate at their customary lot size of four hours' work, we reduced the number of pieces per lot to 10 per cent of customary size (small lots) and timed again. Then we increased slightly to 20 per cent of standard lot size (medium lots). We then returned to the large lot size.

Results were spectacular. The minutes worked between stops during the observation period increased 74 per cent for the small lots as compared with the large ones, with the medium lots intermediate. The number of rest pauses also decreased from large to medium to small lots. There were no changes in output.

Implications for design of work are clear. Since the change of behavior was obtained with no change in monetary incentives, it would be very inexpensive for management to make sure that work is supplied in units of meaningful size, so that workers can feel the pull to complete a task. They also, presumably, can feel the slightly pleasant reward of completing a task, even when the monetary reward system isn't working. What a cheap way to "enrich"! (Baldamus has described other equally promising "tractions." We are waiting for the opportunity to test their effectiveness in field experiments.)

Careful observation and recording of behavior paid off in this study. If, however, we had restricted our thinking to include only those variables that could be conceptualized in the narrow terms of functional analysis, we would never have looked at the spacing of rest pauses as a function of lot size.

INTEGRATE THE INFORMATION

The combination of all of these sources gives us much information, not only from routine tests but also from specialized diagnostic followups. Now we put the picture together to make a diagnosis or several diagnoses. (More than one system may be in trouble.) We consider the way in which causes, strengths and weaknesses interact, so that we understand what is going on and can decide what actions seem most likely to succeed.

RECOMMEND ACTION

At this stage we can push for action, or intervention, to improve the organization. Many actions are possible. We may suggest changes in hiring, in training or promotion programs, in communication, in job design or in other areas. This may even include recommendations for specific behavioral change. But it will also deal with ways to change the beliefs and expectations of all concerned about the system. Changing beliefs is often the most effective of all interventions. (Again, for evidence from the behavior modifiers themselves, see Feeney, 1973; McGinnies, 1970.)

The actions we suggest are not all tender-minded. Sometimes, like the telephone repairman, we have to scrap parts of the system. We have to recommend firing, replacing, transferring or bypassing systems of people which have malfunctioned so long or so severely that they cannot be repaired. Of course, when people are concerned, this decision is made only as a last resort.

Whatever we recommend, we have to be salespeople as well. We present our evidence convincingly, so that the people who receive our information and advice will, after due consideration and discussion, make a wise decision. Sometimes we must recognize that it is not our role to choose which alternative action is better. After all, management and employees alike must make decisions for themselves. But we can give them the bases for choosing soundly.

EVALUATE THE OUTCOMES

Objective evaluation is perhaps the one step that really qualifies us as scientists. We check the results of the action or treatment. Sometimes we find that the action was wrong because our diagnosis was wrong or incomplete. If so, we reassess, gather more information and try again. The process is not mere trial and error. We can, unlike the functional analysts, make some inferences from a finding of no change or no improvement.

REPORT RESULTS

When we think we have succeeded, we translate the results into concrete terms, such as dollars saved or earnings increased. We report results to both employees and management. Employees usually recognize when we have helped their situations, but they appreciate a report about changes that have affected them, and we need to justify the confidence they have placed in us.

For managers, we should turn to the profit and loss statement whenever possible. Translating human behavior into cost-accounting figures is not difficult. It is covered, although not in cookbook form, in such sources as Burns (1972). Actually, a researcher who knows a particular industry well can convert his or her results into dollars and cents saved in absences, turnover, scrap, quality and output, with the enormous concomitant saving on overhead and burden costs. If we are careful to justify our activities in these terms, we are more likely to continue to be supported in activities with less tangible benefits. We will not be regarded as an expendable frill in the organization.

One final word: we can't accomplish anything unless we can operate in an atmosphere of mutual trust. In my opinion, that highly subjective feeling is more important in deciding whether we will be effective in our recommended interventions than all the rigorously scientific devices in our tool kit. In our laboratory, we are trying to develop quantifiable, reliable and valid measures of trust, but until we do so, we can only recommend that management keep in mind that building trust should be a long-term goal. Ethical behavior seems to pay in the long run, or more accurately, even a little unfairness can be immensely costly, because it changes what people *believe*, and a feeling of distrust is very difficult to dispel. Would the counting of frequencies of behaviors as *the* dependent variable, as the bottom line, be likely to increase employees' trust of management or "scientists"?

In summary, I feel that functional analysis is an extremely limited approach. The advocates of the technique have in part imposed the limitations upon themselves, in an attempt to appear more scientific. The consequences have been unfortunate, in failure to know and to use the technical advances in the areas of psychology which they have arbitrarily excluded, such as scaling and psychometrics, moderator variables, individual differences, and training to increase accuracy of observation. They have deprived themselves of important insights. Perhaps more serious is the investigators' inability to assess the relevance of what they do to the needs of organization and its members, or to prove the value of their manipulations.

Instead of relying on fuctional analysis, we should deal with the reasons *why* behavior does or does not occur, with the complex network of measurable (subjective *and* objective) factors which may predict behavior more accurately than either alone. Lawful relationships among beliefs, feelings, intentions, attitudes, abilities and goals are an integral part of a complete and effective psychological science.

Fred Luthans: Thank you, "Shana."[1] I find it very difficult, of course, to argue with apple pie and Pat Smith.[2] I, like everyone else here, greatly respect my opponent. But I think Pat is talking about apples (or apple pie) and I am talking about oranges. The resolution clearly states that we are to discuss organizational behaviors. Yet my opponent initially states that behavior is determined, governed and directed by thoughts, feelings, and values, makes a plea for getting inside of people's heads, and then switches to something called organizational health for the balance of her opening statement. She talks about this "health" in metaphorical terms, such as goals, confidence, cooperation and trust. Who can argue with

---

[1] Editor's note: "Shana" is a reference to the Shana Alexander-James Kilpatrick debates on television called "Point and Counterpoint."

[2] Editor's note: Patricia Cain Smith is widely recognized as a pioneer in industrial psychology and management consulting.

these admirable characteristics of organizations? Certainly not I. But more important to our discussion, who can operationally measure these characteristics, and how are they demonstrably related to organizational behaviors?

I think my opponent has strayed away from the unit of analysis of the resolution and of the field in general. She defines the situation in her own terms, i.e., organizational health, instead of concentrating on observable behaviors and their environmental contingencies. For diagnostic measures of organizational health (not behavior) she suggests both hard data (output, absenteeism, turnover, accidents, earnings and staff) and soft data (perceptions of output to rewards, communication networks, values, beliefs, trust and job satisfaction). She also suggests that we examine work force and organizational characteristics. Then from all of this objective and subjective information we make a diagnosis (presumably of organizational health), evaluate and take action. I can't really argue with this comprehensive approach to macro-organizational analysis. What I do argue with is its relevance to micro-organizational *behaviors*.

The resolution asks for the best way to make a diagnostic evaluation of organizational behavior, not organizational health. I am basing my argument on the significant difference between observable, measurable *behaviors* and unobservable, but nice-sounding and popular, metaphors like *health*. Furthermore, I direct my comments not only to my opponent because she fell into this trap, but also to the field in general to a large extent. I think in many instances we have lost sight of target behaviors. We treat the metaphor (e.g., motivation, satisfaction, leadership or health) as the empirical reality. Yet observable behavior is the empirical reality, isn't it? And what is the best way to make a diagnostic evaluation of it? My opponent would have us examine thoughts, beliefs, trust, feelings and values and "get inside the head of the human being," if you will. I am sorry but I can't do that very well. By having organizational participants fill out a questionnaire or introspect in an interview, I am not sure enough of the reliability and validity of these data to make an effective diagnostic evaluation of their actual behaviors. In other words, I am not willing to rely solely on how an organizational participant "thinks" or "perceives" he or she behaves on the job. I want to see how people actually behave in the ongoing organizational (i.e., naturalistic) setting. If I observe and analyze the environmental contingencies of the behavior through functional analysis, I feel very confident in my ability to predict and control this behavior. Taking the example of Webb et al. (1966), I would rather see dog tracks in the mud than have a thousand sworn testimonies that a dog passed by. It seems to me that functional analysis, which deals with observables, is the best way to make a diagnostic evaluation of organizational *behaviors.* If you ask me the best technique for diagnosing something called organiza- tional *health,* then I think Pat's suggested comprehensive approach certainly has merit.

Pat Smith: Thank you, Fred, for comparing me with something as delicious as apple pie. To address the main arguments, the two most important points for me to make concern the definition of science and the existence of any one "best technique" for all occasions. First, I do not recall any special edict from the gods which permits anyone to define out of existence all procedures that do not meet some narrow criterion of science. To most of us, it is certainly scientific to establish a functional, lawful relationship, whether the behavior is performed by the larger bodily muscles (Fred's "observable behavior") or by movements of the fingers in writing or of the lips, tongue and jaws in speaking (Fred's "subjective reports"). Science includes all, just so long as the variables maintain lawful, consistent, replicable relationships, and so long as those relationships — as you yourself, Fred, pointed out — involve understanding, prediction and control.

About the proposition that there is one "best technique," I'd like to quote from two eminent authors, Mr. Luthans and Mr. Kreitner (1975, p.61):

Too often, however, the behavioral scientist, as a management consultant, has prescribed or pushed for one particular approach or technique without the benefit of an adequate diagnosis. This brings to mind the situation of an unsuspecting patient with an earache who retains the services of a doctor who is bent on performing an appendectomy.

Beautifully said!

Luthans and Kreitner are right. We *do* have to diagnose, and diagnosis is complex. At our university, we spend much of our time teaching students how to see into the interior "works" of an organization, to get its "smell," and to understand what is going on. We also try to teach accurate observation by asking if their observations are confirmed by subjective reports and other measures. We have to teach these complex skills, just as medical schools have to teach their students how to look at the color in a patient's face, the way he stands and walks, the coating on his tongue and all sorts of other subjective observations. It would be malpractice for the physician to avoid such observations, just because they do not lend themselves to a frequency count.

Notice that I am coming out *in favor of* observation. Like mother love (and apple pie), observation of actual behavior is something that all must defend. My own research has emphasized anchoring of judgments and concepts in observed behavior.

I believe observations to be crucial, not because someone proclaims them to be scientific, but because observables such as absences, production and turnover can be linked to organizational goals such as reduced costs and increased profits.

Observation also furnishes subtle cues that may enable us to cross-check whether people are actually behaving as they say they are behaving — or as the observers think they are behaving. Subjective reports, whether made by the *observed employee* or by the *observer,* are frequently the first steps toward a more rigorous scientific formulation. They often represent the end-product of careful observation of the person who sees behavior most frequently — the person himself. They are necessary, moreover, if we are not to bumble around by trial and error. We must not rule them out in an attempt, a superficial attempt, to look scientific. Too much is at stake. We must, instead, work to improve their accuracy.

Two requirements for accuracy must be emphasized. First, observation must be reliable; two observers must agree about what happened, and the reports of behavior must be consistent from time to time. Unfortunately, as I said before, most research on the reliability of any but the most simple (and usually trivial) observations of behavior indicates poor consistency (e.g., Lifson, 1953; Ryan, 1947). Before we naively rely on observation as more scientific than verbal reports, we must concentrate on improving reliability, using the whole repertoire· of technical knowledge gained from research on scaling and on test construction — research which has so far been largely excluded from consideration by most functional analysts.

Second, and more important, observation must be valid. It must be relevant to the subjective feelings and intentions of the person observed. It must be related to the later, long-term behavior which is part of the monetary and non-monetary goals of the person and the organization. When we tally what we observe, we must be sure that we're looking at important and relevant behavior. Otherwise, nose-twitching or finger-lifting is of no interest to us. Since we do have to infer whether a given form of behavior is relevant to either the person or the organization, let's check the accuracy of our inference.

Like observation, offering rewards contingent upon performance is a procedure no scientist could sanely oppose. (No one has, to my knowledge, since 1911 when Franklin Taylor made it one of the foundations of his new Scientific Management programs.)

Because Fred has made such an issue of it, I suppose that I should make it clear that my discussion of diagnosis did *not* represent a shift of topic to organizational health. I have been concerned with organizational variables *only* when they are translated into individual feelings and consequent behavior. I've talked about health because diagnosis, the topic of our debate, concerns health. Organizational health is a composite of the health, broadly defined, of all the individuals that make up the organization; it is indicated by both feelings and behavior.

I must thank Fred for so kindly pointing out for me the circularity of his arguments. It is, indeed, circular to define a reinforcer as some outcome which increases behavior, and then to use as evidence of the causal value of the reinforcer and the scientific approach the fact that the outcome is followed by increases in behavior. The Law of Effect seems to be that what has worked in the past is likely to continue to work — a nice way to freeze the status quo, if you want to do so.

In real life (fortunately for industry and the people in it), the functional analysts don't rely on past history or on trial and error to find out what's reinforcing. They don't say, "Let's try giving workers time off when they increase production and see if they produce more later. If that doesn't work, we will follow each little increase in production with some insurance for dental care and see how that turns out. If that doesn't work . . . '' The practitioners try to be more effective by asking people what they actually want as reinforcers (Luthans and Kreitner, 1975, pp. 93-99). Fred suggested earlier that we "simply ask the person what is a desirable or undesirable consequence." Subjective reports have thus acquired an acknowledged status in behaviorism, even if it is still that of a poor relative.

I cannot repeat too often that there is nothing metaphysical about such concepts as goals, confidence, cooperation and trust. All of these can be expressed clearly in words, and all have been shown to be related to important behavior. Especially valuable is the subjective (but not metaphysical) self-report of intention to behave, or intention to achieve a goal. This self-report, I remind you, is an effective predictor of behavior. Hence, the measurement of goals and intentions is not only a quick but also an efficient way to anticipate behavior.

It is a major goal of research and training to increase the accuracy of such measurements. It is an important and challenging scientific puzzle to disentangle the complex web of their interrelationships.

Above all, in our search for truth, for control and understanding, we should not handicap ourselves by the tunnel vision imposed by a narrow, doctrinaire belief about what is scientific. We should survey all the available evidence, thoroughly and systematically. And we must strive for true understanding. It is a necessary element in organizational and managerial decisions, as well as a response to the human search to know, Why?

Fred Luthans: Pat seems mainly concerned that functional analysis is only one approach, not necessarily the best, and that it is not the only scientific approach. I am taking the position that functional analysis is the best way to make a diagnostic evaluation of organizational behavior. It is obviously not the only, nor necessarily the most popular, approach. Attempting to make subjective causal attributions that occur inside of people's heads or asking people to fill out standardized questionnaries describing their thoughts, beliefs, feelings, trusts and values is certainly an alternative approach, but it does not seem to be as effective as systematic analysis of the observable environmental contingencies of the behavior in question. However, I would also quickly add that I don't quarrel with the comprehensive approach utilizing both hard and soft measures that Pat advocates for diagnosing organizational *health*. But, as I said earlier, our resolution is aimed at behavior, not the metaphor "health." A focus on behaviors permits us to be grounded in empirical reality. As Mintzberg (1973, 1975) and others have pointed out, there are a lot of myths and misrepresentations about managerial work and organizational life. By concentrating on ongoing behaviors, instead of nice-sounding but often elusive and nonexistent metaphors such as health, climate or trust, we should be much more efficient and productive in our diagnostic evaluations.

As for Pat's contention that subjective techniques for measuring nonobservables are just as scientific as functional analysis for measuring observables is a debatable issue that we will not resolve here. I fully realize that many people interested in the philosophy of science feel that there should be different rules for accumulating knowledge and searching for truth in different disciplines. I guess I am old-fashioned in that respect. I like to think that we are *striving* to attain a science of organizational behavior with the *goal* of true functional laws. Notice, I used the words "striving" and "goal." I do not think we have a science of organizational behavior yet, nor true functional laws in the tradition of the Law of Effect. But I do think this is how we should proceed. By stressing the need to use (1) observable behaviors as the unit of analysis and (2) functional analysis, which depends on observable environmental contingencies, as the best technique for diagnostic evaluation, I am espousing the scientific methodology of operationalism. I do not deny the existence of inner, mediating variables or their role in human behavior in organizations. In fact, my past, present and future writings always do and will give specific recognition to nonobservable, mediating variables. For example, I think that an S-O-R (stimulus-operant-response) paradigm is more representative of human behavior than is a mechanistically based S-R (stimulus-response) paradigm. I am currently working on studies that draw heavily from social learning theory and deal specifically with covert, unobservable variables. I think that an important area for future theory building, research and application in organizational behavior will be found in the implications of self-control, which definitely involves nonobservables. I also think there is a desperate need to develop systematic, indirect, observational techniques to prove the existence of nonobservables. The sensory preconditioning experiments in psychology and, of course, the work done in genetics and physics are examples of such techniques. In other words, I do not feel that I am taking an extreme position; I certainly do not consider myself a radical behaviorist. Obviously, I agree with a great deal of what Pat says. But I do take the position that in this resolution and in the field in general, observable behavior should be the *primary* (not only) emphasis, not metaphors such as organizational health, climate or trust, which seem to me often to become ends in themselves. And I do object to the almost sole reliance on standardized questionnaires to gather data on the metaphors. I think we need a return to operationalism, with its emphasis on measuring observables. In other words, I believe that functional analysis is indeed the best available technique for the diagnostic evaluation of organizational behavior.

Pat Smith: I think we're really in agreement about a great deal. We agree about the desirability of apple pie, science, observation of behavior and attempts at a clear diagnosis (although we disagree about what some of these terms mean). We also oppose all sins such as merely relating two reports from the same observer (e.g., relating one questionnaire response to another) and, presumably, cheating at cards.

But I think I should take one more whack at the importance of *under-standing.* Interpreting correlational data without *understanding* is an evil, whatever point of view we take. For example, I have a beautiful new set of analyses of data from an old study which would seem to demonstrate, by a very high correlation, that the way to improve the satisfaction of men in a plant is to raise the women's salaries. Some might naively infer this conclusion from the correlation of means across a number of plants. It's consistent, it's replicable, and it's a law. Nuts! It's an artifact, and you know it and I know it. This kind of scientific error would not be corrected by knowing whether the mean women's salaries also correlate with observable *behavior,* for example, the men's rates of absence. Because I cannot probe beneath the observables in this case, I do not consider the relationship a scientific fact. That is what I mean by the necessity for understanding.

It is extremely important, whatever approach we use, that we keep the total picture in mind. We have to continue to be clear about the goals we are trying to achieve and about how our research investigations are related to those goals. We, like those we study, are human beings. Let us, therefore, try to act in ways that at least appear to be insightful, thoughtful, well-organized and integrative. Let us use all our resources to be effective persons, both as scientists and as practitioners.

REFERENCES AND RECOMMENDED READINGS (Luthans).

Azrin, N.H., Holz, W., and Goldiamod, I. Response bias in questionnaire reports, *Journal of Consulting Psychology,* 1961, *25,* 324-326.

Bandura, A. *Social Learning Theory.* Englewood Cliffs, N.J.: Prentice-Hall, 1977.

Carpenter, F. *The Skinner Primer: Behind Freedom and Dignity.* New York: The Free Press, 1974.

Conversation with B.F. Skinner. *Organizational Dynamics,* Winter 1973, 31-40.

Cummings, L.L., Behling, O.C., Luthans, F., Nord, W. R. and Mitchell, T. R. Reinforcement analysis in management: concepts, issues, and controversies: A symposium. *Organization and Administrative Science,* Spring 1976, 41-72.

Deese, J. *Psychology as Science and Art.* New York: Harcourt, Brace, Jovanovich, 1972.

Fry, F. Operant conditioning and O.B. Mod.: of mice and men. *Personnel,* July-August 1974, 17-24.

Jablonsky, S. F. and DeVries, D. L. Operant conditioning principles extrapolated to the theory of management. *Organizational Behavior and Human Performance,* 1972, *7,* 340-358.

Keller, F. S. *Learning: Reinforcement Theory.* New York: Random House, 1954.

Locke, E. A. The myths of behavior mod in organizations. *Academy of Management Review,* 1977, *2,* 543-553.

Luthans, F. Applied behavioral analysis and change, in *Organizational Behavior.* New York: McGraw-Hill, 1977, Chapter 20.

Luthans, F. and Kreitner, R. The management of behavioral contingencies. *Personnel,* July-August 1974, 7-16.

Luthans, F. and Kreitner, R. *Organizational Behavior Modification.* Glenview, Ill. Scott, Foresman, 1975.

Luthans, F. and Ottemann, R. Motivation vs. learning approaches to organizational behavior. *Business Horizons,* December 1973, 55-62.

Mahoney, M. J. *Cognition and Behavior Modification.* Cambridge, Mass.: Ballinger, 1974.

Mawhinney, T. C. Operant terms and concepts in the description of individual work behavior: some problems of interpretation, application, and evaluation. *Journal of Applied Psychology,* 1975, *60,* 704-712.

McGinnies, E. *Social Behavior: A Functional Analysis.* Boston: Houghton Mifflin, 1970.

Mintzberg, H. *The Nature of Managerial Work.* New York: Harper and Row, 1973.

Mintzberg, H. The manager's job: folklore and fact, *Harvard Business Review,* July-August, 1975, *53,* 49-61.

Nord, W. Beyond the teaching machine: the neglected area of operant conditioning in the theory and practice of management. *Organizational Behavior and Human Performance,* 1969, *4,* 375-401.

Premack, D. Reinforcement theory, in D. Levine (Ed.): *Nebraska Symposium on Motivation,* Lincoln, Nebraska: University of Nebraska, 1965, 123-180.

Reynolds, G. S. *A Primer of Operant Conditioning,* Rev. Ed. Glenview, Ill. Scott, Foresman, 1975.

Rogers, C. and Skinner, B. F. Some issues concerning the control of human behavior. *Science,* 1956, *124,* 1057-1066.

Schneier, C. E. Behavior modification in management: a review and critique. *Academy of Management Journal,* 1974, *17,* 528-548.

Skinner, B. F. *Science and Human Behavior.* New York: The Free Press, 1953.

Skinner, B. F. *Contingencies of Reinforcement.* New York: Appleton-Century Crofts, 1969.

Skinner, B. F. The steep and thorny way to a science of behavior. *American Psychologist,* 1975, *30,* 42-49.

Webb, E. J., Campbell, D. T., Schwartz, R. D. and Sechrest, L. *Unobtrusive Measures.* Chicago: Rand McNally, 1966.

REFERENCES AND RECOMMENDED READINGS (Smith)

Badia, P. and Culbertson, S, The relative aversiveness of signalled vs. unsignalled escapable and inescapable shock. *The Journal of the Experimental Analysis of Behavior,* 1972, *17,* 463-471.

Baldamus, W. Incentives and work analysis. *University of Birmingham Studies in Economics and Society,* 1951, Monograph A1, 1-78.

Besco, R. O. and Lawshe, C. H. Foreman leadership as perceived by superiors and subordinates. *Personnel Psychology,* 1959, *12,* 573-582.

Burns, T. J. (Ed.). *Behavioral Experiments in Accounting.* Columbus: Ohio State University Press, 1972.

Feeney, E. J. At Emery Air Freight: positive reinforcement boosts performance. *Organizational Dynamics,* 1973, *1,* 41-50.

Guion, R. M. Recruiting, selection and job placement, in M.D. Dunnette (Ed.): *Handbook of Industrial and Organizational Psychology.* Chicago: Rand McNally, 1976, 777-828.

Guion, R. M. and Smith, P.C. Motivation, in H. L. Fromkin and J. J. Sherwood (Eds.): *Integrating the Organization.* New York: The Free Press, 1974, 154-176.

Hinrichs, J. R. Personnel training, in M.D. Dunnette (Ed.): *Handbook of Industrial and Organizational Psychology.* Chicago: Rand McNally, 1976, 829-860.

Kraut, A. I. Predicting turnover of employees from measured job attitudes. *Organizational Behavior and Human Performance,* 1975, *13,* 233-243.

Landy, F. J. and Trumbo, D. A. *Psychology of Work Behavior.* Homewood, Ill. Dorsey, 1976.

La Rocco, J.M., Pugh, W. M. and Gunderson, E. K. E. Identifying determinants of retention decisions. *Personnel Psychology,* 1977, *30,* 199-216.

Latham, G. P., Mitchell, T. R. and Dossett, D. L. Importance of participative goal setting and anticipated rewards on goal difficulty and job performance. *Journal of Applied Psychology,* 1978, *63,* 163-171.

Latham, G. P. and Yukl, G. A. A review of research on the application of goal setting in organizations. *Academy of Management Journal,* 1975a, *18,* 824-845.

Latham, G. P. and Yukl, G. A. Assigned versus participative goal setting with educated and uneducated woods workers. *Journal of Applied Psychology,* 1975b, *60,* 299-302.

Latham, G. P. and Yukl, G. A. The effects of assigned and participative goal setting on performance and job satisfaction. *Journal of Applied Psychology,* 1976, *61,* 166-177.

Lifson, K. A. Errors in time-study judgments of industrial work pace. *Psychological Monographs,* 1953, *67,* No. 5 (Whole No. 355).

Locke, E. A. Toward a theory of task motivation and incentives. *Organizational Behavior and Human Performance,* 1968, *3,* 157-189.

Luthans, F. and Kreitner, R. *Organizational Behavior Modification.* Glenview, Ill.: Scott, Foresman, 1975.

McCormick, E. J. Job and task analysis, in M.D. Dunnette (Ed.): *Handbook of Industrial and Organizational Psychology.* Chicago: Rand McNally, 1976, 651-696.

McGinnies, E. *Social Behavior: A Functional Analysis.* Boston: Houghton Mifflin, 1970.

Mathewson, S. B. *Restriction of Output among Unorganized Workers.* New York: Viking Press, 1931.

Price, J. L. *Handbook of Organizational Measurement.* Lexington, Mass.: Heath, 1972.

The Random House Dictionary of the English Language. New York: Random House, 1973.

Roethlisberger, F. J. and Dixon, W. J. *Management and the Worker.* Cambridge, Mass.: Harvard University Press, 1939.

Rothe, H. F. Output rates among industrial employees. *Journal of Applied Psychology,* 1978, *63,* 40-46.

Ryan, T. A. *Work and Effort.* New York, Ronald, 1947.

Ryan, T. A. *Intentional Behavior: An Approach to Human Motivation.* New York: Ronald, 1970.

Ryan, T. A. and Smith, P. C. *Principles of Industrial Psychology.* New York: Ronald, 1954.

Smith, P. C. The curve of output as a criterion of boredom. *Journal of Applied Psychology,* 1953, *37,* 69-74.

Smith, P. C. Behaviors, results and organizational effectiveness: the problem of criteria, in M.D. Dunnette (Ed.): *Handbook of Industrial and Organizational Psychology.* Chicago: Rand McNally, 1976, 745-776.

Smith, P.C., and Lem, C. Positive aspects of motivation in repetitive work: effects of lot size upon spacing of voluntary work stoppages. *Journal of Applied Psychology,* 1955, *39,* 330-333.

Smith, P. C. and Smith, O. W. Review of F. Luthans and R. Kreitner: *Organizational Behavior Modification.* Glenview, Ill. Scott, Foresman, 1975, in *Personnel Psychology,* 1976, *29,* 122-124.

Smith, P.C., Kendall, L. M. and Hulin, C. L. *The Measurement of Satisfaction in Work and Retirement: A Strategy for the Study of Attitudes.* Chicago: Rand McNally, 1969.

Taylor, F. W. *The Principles of Scientific Management.* New York: Harper, 1911.

Wollack, S. Goodale, J. G., Wijting, J. P. and Smith, P.C. Development of the Survey of Work Values. *Journal of Applied Psychology,* 1971, *55,* 331-338.

Zedeck, S. and Baker, H. T. Nursing performance as measured by behavioral expectation scales: a multitrait-multirater analysis. *Organizational Behavior and Human Performance,* 1972, *7,* 457-466.

Zedeck, S. and Blood, M. R. *Foundations of Behavioral Science Research in Organizations.* Monterey, Ca.: Brooks/Cole, 1974.

Zedeck, S. and Smith, P.C. A psychophysical determination of equitable payment. *Journal of Applied Psychology,* 1968, *52,* 343-347.

Chapter 5

TASK DESIGN

INTRODUCTION

From the practical orientation of the last debate we turn to a number of questions about research methodology and meaning. The domain is task design, but the conceptual problem, dealing with individual differences, is a thorn in the paw of all OB researchers. If this metaphor conjures up for you an image of a mighty lion limping slowly because of a wee thorn, you are correct. But we suspect that it will take more than a mouse to remove this thorn.[1]

In this chapter the debaters engage in a discussion of "modeling," that is, conceptual mapping of the way variables might fit together. One debater charges that the conceptual map (analytical model) that underlies most research on task design is both oversimplistic and wrongfully applied. It is notable that few journal articles and few classroom discussions attempt to dig under the surface of research studies to examine underlying models. This chapter, then, provides a much-needed reminder of the value of this examination and an example of how to go about it. Doctoral students, take note.

Since this chapter frequently uses technical terms in research methodology, the reader would be well advised to refresh himself or herself on the meaning of such terms as independent, moderating and dependent variables, explained variance, and subjective perceptions versus objective characteristics. The glossary at the end of this book will help with some of these terms.

The domain in which the individual differences battle is waged in this book is task design, otherwise known as job scope, the design of work or task attributes. Because Ed Lawler plunges into the domain in his opening comments, the beginning student should first consult a basic textbook. The bulk of existing research on task design assumes that individuals have varying levels of growth need strength (see glossary) and thus respond differently to their jobs. In addition, this body of research attempts to identify the particular elements, or attributes, of jobs that are associated with individual preferences. The

---

[1] Reference is made to the ancient fable in which a tiny mouse saves the life of a thorn-crippled lion.

most commonly mentioned attributes of tasks are variety, autonomy, meaningfulness (significance), identity (wholeness) and feedback. It is presumed that jobs that possess high levels of these characteristics are enriching for workers and will lead to better attitudes and higher performance levels—**if** the individual worker desires enrichment. This presumption and the methodological problems that surround its investigation are the meat of the debate between these friendly rivals, Lawler and Cummings. The debate is shorter than others in this book, but do not be deceived. Its brevity does not imply that it is easy or superficial. Dig in!

A final comment on the relationship between this debate and the other three. In this chapter you will find no explicit language dealing with cognitive versus behavioristic assumptions about the nature of man. There are, however, many ways in which that general theme is implicit in the remarks of these debaters. An attempt to identify these underlying assumptions will serve as an applied test of comprehension of concepts discussed earlier.

EDWARD E. LAWLER, III

Edward E. Lawler III is Professor of Organizational Behavior at the University of Southern California. After graduating from the University of California at Berkeley in 1964, Dr. Lawler joined the faculty of the University of Michigan at Ann Arbor, becoming Professor of Industrial Administration and Psychology. Since 1975, Dr. Lawler has been director of the Organizational Behavior Program at the Institute of Social Research at the University. He is also a Visiting Scientist at the Human Affairs Research Center at the Battelle Memorial Institute in Seattle, Washington.

Resolved: Individual differences add explained variance in predicting the outcomes of task design.

Barbara Karmel: Our speaker for the affirmative of this resolution is Edward E. Lawler, III and for the negative is Larry L. Cummings.

Ed Lawler: Thank you, Barbara. One day last winter I was presented with an invitation that required me to make an interesting decision. Barbara called to ask if I would participate in this debate. I had already assessed myself as having relatively strong growth needs; therefore, it was a matter of analyzing the task to determine if its characteristics were a good fit with my growth needs. A careful look at the task indicated that certainly there was plenty of autonomy. With a bright, enthusiastic, active audience like this, I was assured of feedback. Where I paused for a moment was on the issue of meaningfulness. The position I was asked to support seemed so clear-cut, the weight of empirical evidence so much on my side, it was hard for me to imagine there *could* be a debate which would indeed tax my skills and abilities to the point where it

He is the author and coauthor of many books and articles in his field, including *Motivation in Work Organizations*, published by Brooks-Cole Publishing Company in 1973. With Porter and Hackman he coauthored *Behavior in Organizations*, published by McGraw-Hill in 1975. Dr. Lawler is a fellow of the Academy of Management and a member of the American Psychological Association.

would satisfy my growth needs. Then Barbara threw in the clincher: she said Larry Cummings would be my opponent, and I said to myself if there were anyone who could make a silk purse out of a sow's ear, it was Larry. In the face of little supporting evidence, no logic and no basis for his argument, I was sure that he could make the debate interesting. Thus I decided to take on the task.

A review of the literature indicated that my original diagnosis of the situation was entirely correct. The evidence is almost 100 per cent on my side. I found eight studies that looked at the issue of whether individuals with strong growth needs respond differently to jobs than do individuals with weak growth needs (see Hackman, 1977, for a review of most of these). They all show that for high-growth-need individuals there is a stronger relationship between job design characteristics and such outcomes as satisfaction and motivation than there is for weak-growth-need individuals. Seven of the studies are correlational; one is an experimental study. Several studies have looked at individual difference factors other than growth need strength. One looked at intrinsic work values, and it also found a moderating effect. One has compared a series of different moderators, finding all of them to have an effect, but growth needs were shown to be the best moderator variable.

The only studies that have shown mixed results are those which have made a methodological leap by using sociological level variables like urban-rural background in order to try to get a psychological variable, internal need states of individuals. Those studies have had mixed success, about 50 per cent showing successful moderator variable effects, and 50 per cent showing unsuccessful moderator variable effects. This should hardly be surprising given that the variable urban-rural is so far removed from what seems to be the underlying causal variable, need strength.

Despite the research that has been done, there is a pressing need for more work on how individual difference variables affect people's reactions to different job designs. I would like to see some research on variables such as age, previous job history and education to determine their impact on individuals' reactions to different job designs. I suspect that those would show some consistent effects. I would also like to see research on the long-term effects on growth need strength that result from exposing individuals to different types of job design.

Finally, I would like to concede that there are some methodological problems in looking at moderator variables. Indeed, many recent articles have been written about this. However, I'm convinced by the overwhelming consistency of the evidence that individual differences *do* make a difference. I ask you, do all people want a great deal of autonomy, or variety, or meaningfulness embedded in their jobs? Do some people want to achieve a sense of autonomy in off-the-job activities? Do some people have less total need for autonomy than others?

I would suggest, therefore, that we concentrate on thinking about how we can help organizations design work for *individuals,* so that improvements can be made in the fit between the needs of individuals and the way jobs are designed. I don't think anyone can deny that the lack of fit is a serious problem in this country. It often results in dissatisfaction, low motivation, absenteeism and turnover. In order to correct this situation, we must accept the fact that people differ and get on with our task of helping oganizations to design jobs that are well-suited to people's individual needs.

Larry Cummings: If we are to undertake a systematic analysis of the

LARRY L. CUMMINGS

Larry L. Cummings is a professor and H.I. Romnes Faculty Fellow in the Graduate School of Business, University of Wisconsin-Madison. He teaches and does research in the areas of organizational behavior, organizational theory, personnel and management.

Dr. Cummings recently completed his term as editor of the *Academy of Management Journal,* and is the coauthor and editor of three books: *Readings in Organizational Behavior and Human Performance* (1969, 1973); *Organizational Decision Making* (1970) and *Performance in Organizations* (1973). He has published more than 60 articles and is a fellow of the Academy of Management and the American Psychological Association. He was recently elected Vice President Program Chairman of the Academy.

importance of individual differences in explaining behavior, I think there are four central issues to which we must attend. The first concerns the selection of an appropriate analytical framework for resolving the issues. As stated, the resolution implies that individual differences are to be thought of as independent variables in a causal design.

Individual Differences

(Diagram A)

Differences in Attitude
and Behavior Outcomes

Alternatively, and the way that Ed has chosen to interpret it, one might conceive of such differences as moderators of the relationship between job design, on the one hand, and some kind of dependent variable of interest, on the other.

Job Design

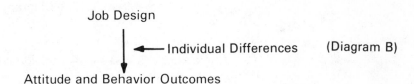

Individual Differences   (Diagram B)

Attitude and Behavior Outcomes

The analytical framework and the techniques appropriate for investigation of each of these two models are quite different, and they are often confused in the literature. There is *no* clear evidence that individual differences (IDs) add anything to explained variance as independent variables. In fact, it has not even been tested. Most of the designs and analytical models have been aimed at discovering "under what conditions" variations in task designs impact on some dependent variable. Past studies have not been designed to evaluate effects on explained variance.

The second issue focuses on the way individual differences *have* been studied. Which of the formulations that I have presented has been predominant in the literature? And have implications been derived from one perspective and applied incorrectly to another? I think much of the evidence from moderator analyses has been summarized, and even used to make prescriptions, by treating individual differences as an independent variable, and inappropriately so.

Thirdly, regardless of the analytical model that has been utilized, individual differences have been positioned in a framework between perceptions of the task on the one hand and attitudinal and behavioral responses on the other. A major step forward, and I think the really important one in any job design model, would be to link objective task characteristics directly to perceptions of that task. Individual differences have not been studied in this way by organizational behavior scholars, either as (1) determinants of such perceptions, or (2) moderators of the objective perceived task characteristics. (See Diagram C1 and C2.)

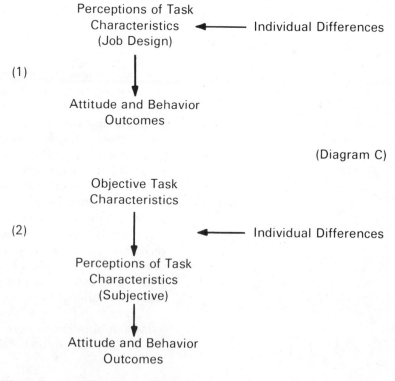

(1)

Perceptions of Task
    Characteristics ◄——————— Individual Differences
    (Job Design)
        │
        ▼
Attitude and Behavior
    Outcomes

(Diagram C)

(2)

Objective Task
Characteristics
        │
        ▼ ◄——————— Individual Differences
Perceptions of Task
Characteristics
(Subjective)
        │
        ▼
Attitude and Behavior
    Outcomes

There is little evidence available on which to make an affirmative case that individual differences impact upon how tasks are perceived. Mostly, the evidence indicates that perceptions of tasks, perceptions of needs and perceptions of attitude and behavior outcomes are correlated. However, perception-perception correlations do not constitute evidence that IDs add explained variance.

Finally, regardless of the analytical and conceptual models used, is there any substantial, accumulative, systematic evidence that individual differences add any explained variance? While the literature leaves much to be desired analytically, it generally supports my position, the negative of the resolution. Kenneth White, in a paper to be published in *Academy of Management Review*,[1] has reviewed 29 studies, *not* 8. He concludes that: (1) very often, no moderating effects are found; (2) when moderators are found, they are highly inconsistent; (3) the real situation is probably worse than that, because nonsignificant findings are probably never published; and (4) at best, moderators can be expected to hold up only for narrowly defined constructs and specific samples and situations. Thus, the research history contained in this review of roughly 30 studies has not provided much evidence that is useful for generalizing or claiming that increases in explained variance result from accounting for individual differences.

Ed Lawler: I'd like to pick up on the issue of explained variance. It's true that studies have tended not to look at a direct correlation between people's responses to jobs and individual needs (Diagram A, above). Indeed, there is no theoretical reason for that to occur. On the other hand, when you can take a moderator

---

[1]Since published. See References and Recommended Readings.

variable and increase the percentage of explained variance by anywhere from 7 to 30 per cent, which the studies *have* done, I think that is increasing the explained variance. Just the ability to partition a sample into groups (one having high explained variance and the other having low explained variance) to me, at least, does lead to an increase in explained variance. Now, we could get into the semantics of whether that is due to the individual difference effects or not. I would argue that it *is* due to the individual difference effects.

I particularly appreciated Larry's comment that even though we have a lot of evidence on the positive side, we've got to take into account all those unpublished studies. One answer to that is, if we could only straighten out those journal editors[1] and get them to publish nonsignificant results, we'd be able to do an objective count of the actual ratio of successful to unsuccessful studies supporting this position. I haven't been successful myself in straightening them out; maybe this debate, if nothing else, will have that impact.

As far as looking at the objective task characteristics, I think Larry was a little too quick in suggesting that we don't have any evidence on objective task characteristics. Indeed, I've done several studies, and there are others in the literature that have looked at task characteristics as assessed by an observer and have compared them with individual perceptions of the same task characteristics. Typically, a positive relationship has been found between these two assessments of task characteristics.

I feel a bit sandbagged when Larry refers to a yet-to-be-published study in the *Academy of Management Review,* since it is very difficult for me to know whether

---

[1]Editor's note: Lawler refers to the fact that his opponent in the debate, Cummings, was at that time Editor of the *Academy of Management Journal.*

those 29 studies really looked at the kind of individual difference variables that *should* make the difference as moderators of job design. I don't think we can assume that all individual difference variables will moderate the relationship between task characteristics and outcomes such as motivation and satisfaction, nor am I sure that exactly the same variables will work in all situations. Indeed, if there is any area for future research, I would say it's getting on with the issue of identifying which individual difference variables do act as moderators and determining *why* they act as moderators (Diagram B, above). I agree we could push a little harder on the issue of objective task characteristics versus subjective ones, and how individual difference variables may moderate the relationship between objective task characteristics and subjective task characteristics (Diagram C, above). There is some evidence from the research on achievement motivation which shows, in fact, that need strength may impact on subjective task characteristics, and I think this could be an interesting area for future research.

Larry Cummings: The forthcoming article that I mentioned references only previously published studies; those are completely available in the literature.

The second point is that the average addition, the mean addition, to explained variance in those studies (Ed's eight is presumably a subset of those), is roughly 5 per cent. Where Ed gets the 30 per cent I'm not sure. Thirdly, there is also a study that has been widely circulated in the prepublication network and is in press at present, which shows that in 14 research sites, all 73 potential moderators fall into the three major classifications that Ed refers to. These are not wild, far-out types of moderators, higher order need strength and urban-rural characteristics being examples. In this review, there is not one moderator that holds up across the 14 research sites.

Finally, I would make the general point that the problem with looking at individual difference moderators in this context is that most of the time we're going to find that the effects of individual difference moderators, if any at all, would be associated with very trivial kinds of environmental stimulation. That is, we would expect such moderators to add substantially to explained variance only when there are fairly trivial differences in the design of tasks.

Ed Lawler: Let me summarize my position by looking at what happens if we accept the assumption that individual differences don't make a difference. It seems to me that if we make that assumption, we then come back to arguing that it really doesn't matter what jobs individuals are placed in, that we should merely assign people to jobs because everyone will like and be motivated by all jobs equally. I would argue that this contradicts not only the research evidence (and I must admit I haven't seen the other unpublished study that Larry is familiar with) but also my experience.

Time after time, people tell me that they wouldn't have my job for all the money in the world, and I tell them that I wouldn't have theirs for all the money in the world. Maybe this isn't an individual difference factor operating, but something seems to be going on there. In addition, people constantly sort themselves out among jobs on some basis that at least seems to indicate there are meaningful, consistent individual differences. For example, I recently did a study of a change in which people were given a chance to volunteer for enriched jobs or to stay on their traditional jobs. Half of the people volunteered for the enriched jobs; the other half stayed on their old jobs. The change agents were distraught and destroyed; their pet had been rejected by half of the people. They couldn't believe it. My argument was that they had made 50 per cent of the individuals' lives better, and no one's worse — wasn't that good enough? In terms of the "explained variance" theme of this resolution, there would seem to be no question that the personal preferences of these workers (individual differences) would affect their performance and motivation (attitude and behavioral outcomes) on redesigned, enriched jobs. This effect *is* an addition to explained variance. Our task, then, is to find the right moderators, identify the situations in which the moderating effect occurs, and develop valid measurement instruments that are sensitive to these effects.

Larry Cummings: I'd make four points in summary. First, our thinking is not clear about the difference between (a) discovering those persons for whom perceptions of the task design and attitudinal outcomes are correlated versus those persons for whom there is no correlation, and (b) adding to the variance explained within either of those subgroups. Secondly, I think incorrect implications and conclusions are being drawn from findings about the former kind of study and applied incorrectly to the latter kind of study. Thirdly, at a conceptual level, individual differences have played a very minor role in building a model of task design effects. They've been studied almost solely in terms of a perception-perception nexus, and thus we can draw no conclusions from the research about their role in helping us to explain responses to environmental variations in task design.

A more complete and defensible model would distinguish between objective characteristics and individuals' *perceptions* of those characteristics. The following diagram graphically represents this distinction and the potential for interaction between objective and perceptual characteristics. Research studies to date have, by and large, neglected to take these factors into account.

(Diagram D)

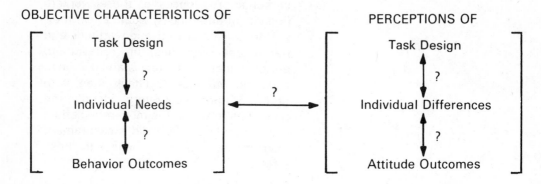

OBJECTIVE CHARACTERISTICS OF

Task Design

?

Individual Needs

?

Behavior Outcomes

?

PERCEPTIONS OF

Task Design

?

Individual Differences

?

Attitude Outcomes

Note that these linkages are as yet unspecified because the majority of research has been based on simplistic and indefensible analytical models.

Finally, even if we ignore the fact that most studies have measured perception-perception correlations (a charge of false-positive leaving the research open to challenge), there is *still* little evidence to indicate that additional variance in responses is explained. It is the familiar tempest in a teapot. Let us get on with the measurement and evaluation of actual objective characteristics of the task, and then identify an analytical framework which will lead to real understanding of the implications of task design and job content.

REFERENCES AND RECOMMENDED READINGS

Davis, L. E. and Taylor, R. N. *The Design of Work*. London: Penguin, 1972.
Hackman, J. R. Work design, in J. R. Hackman and J. L. Suttle (Eds.): *Improving Life at Work: Behavioral Science Approaches to Organizational Change*. Santa Monica, Ca.: Goodyear, 1977.
Hackman, J. R. and Lawler, E. E., III. Employee reactions to job characteristics. *Journal of Applied Psychology*, 1971, *55*, 259-286.
Hackman, J. R. and Oldham, G. R. Development of the job diagnostic survey. *Journal of Applied Psychology*, 1975, *60*, 159-170.

Herzberg, F. One more time: How do you motivate employees? *Harvard Business Review*, January-February 1968, *46*, No. 1, 53-62.

Herzberg, F., Mausner, B. and Snyderman, B. *The Motivation to Work*. New York: Wiley and Sons, 1959.

Lawler, E. E. *Motivation in Work Organizations*. Monterey, Ca.: Brooks/Cole, 1973.

Lawler, E. E. The individualized organization: Problems and promise. *California Management Review*, 1974, *17*, 31-39.

Pierce, J. L. and R. B. Dunham. Task design: a literature review. *Academy of Management Review*, 1976, *1*, 3-97.

Smith, P.C., Kendall, L. M. and Hulin, C. L. *Measurement of Satisfaction in Work and Retirement*. New York: Rand McNally, 1969.

Wanous, J. P. Individual differences and reactions to job characteristics. *Journal of Applied Psychology*, 1974, *59*, 616-622.

White, J. K. Generalizability of individual difference moderators of the participation in decision-making-employee response relationship. *Academy of Management Journal*, 1978a, *21*, 36-43.

White, J. K. Individual differences and the job-quality worker response relationship: Review, integration and comments. *Academy of Management Review*, April 1978b, *3*, 267-280.

Chapter 6

LEADERSHIP

INTRODUCTION

We now move from an emphasis on methodological frameworks in the last chapter to hard core expositions of two specific theoretical propositions: reinforcement theory and path goal theory. The term "hard core" is used deliberately to forewarn the reader to take, as we say out west, a deep seat and a short rein. It will help if you review expectancy and instrumentality and their evolution into path goal theory before commencing this chapter. Similarly, a basic review of operant principles will be beneficial.

Armed wtih the necessary vocabulary, you will find the remarks of these two debators a veritable treatise on the state of the art in leadership and motivation. You will be treated by both men to numerous illustrations from real life, ranging from snake phobias and rat behavior to driver training and the development of subordinate confidence. Evans will cite a particular research study and offer four alternative interpretations that might be proposed by behaviorists. He will argue that these interpretations are incorrect and provide a rationale for his position.

These contributions notwithstanding, the most important element of the debate is an unadorned presentation of the boundaries between behaviorists and cognitive psychologists. You will see the debators come up against these boundaries, glance off in some cases, invade some portions of each other's territory to borrow concepts, but conclude that they are *not* saying the same things, that their differences are not simply semantic. This is described by one debator as a paradigm conflict, a conflict that may generate the enormous research energy needed to seek synthesis. It is your editor's humble opinion that this debate and others like it, conducted in seminars and classrooms, will lead to a new generation of research in OB.

One final word before you go to work with Drs. Scott and Evans: The resolution is worded in the negative to maintain a balance between behavioristic and cognitive hypotheses expressed in the four resolutions. Hence, Bill Scott will argue the affirmative, a behavioristic position, and Marty Evans will argue the negative of the resolution, a cognitive perspective. For fun, you may want to read the last sentence of the debate first.

WILLIAM E. SCOTT, JR.

Dr. Scott is a Professor of Organizational Behavior in the Graduate School of Business at Indiana University and serves on the Editorial Boards of the *Journal of Organizational Behavior and Human Performance* and the *Journal of Organizational Behavior Management.* He is best known for his "activation theory" of task design and for his early and continued emphasis upon a reinforcement analysis of organizational behavior. His most recent work includes an experimental analysis of "intrinsic motivation," an arousal interpretation of reinforcement effects, a functional analysis of leadership behavior and a forthcoming book on behavioral principles for organizational leaders.

Dr. Scott is a member of the Academy of Management, American Psychological Association and Sigma Xi.

Resolved: Expectancy and expectation are *not* central concepts in leadership research.

Bill Scott: I interpret this resolution to mean the following: There are theorists who contend that some sort of inner process or thing called an "expectancy" is among the root causes of the behavior we observe on the job. I make no such claim, of course, but my esteemed colleague (Evans, 1968) has postulated that behavior is importantly determined by the cognition that a particular path (behavior) will lead to given outcomes or goals[1] and that the individual assesses those goals as valent. Furthermore, both Evans and House (1971) have postulated that organizational leaders, by behaving in certain ways, are capable of changing the expectancies of their subordinates and, hence, the behavior presumably governed by those inner processes or events. House (1971), for example, has noted that if a leader consistently rewards a certain class of behavior ambiguously described as "achievement," then he or she will most probably increase the subordinate's path instrumentality or expectancy that such behavior will lead to valent personal outcomes. Curiously, the question of what causes the behavior of *leaders* is not addressed by either Evans or House, although both would quite probably argue that the behavior of leaders is also caused by expectations or instrumentalities.

---

[1]Evans has called this cognition a "path instrumentality" which, he notes, is akin to, but not identical with, an expectancy. However, one must question the assertion that the two concepts are different, since Vroom (1964, p. 17) has defined an expectancy as the momentary *belief* that a given act will be followed by a given outcome.

My most fundamental objection to the expectancy concept is that it has been examined and found wanting on several grounds, all of which indicate that it reflects the fallacy of concept reification. The fallacy is in assuming that whenever we emit a single noun word such as "expectancy," there is inevitably something in nature which corresponds with the word, something as real and as readily entering into subject-predicate relations with other things as the noun itself. When, for example, we announce for the benefit of another person that "Barbara[1] shoved her brother over the rail," the word "Barbara" is a stimulus event, as much a part of our environment as the ticking of a metronome. 'Barbara" is also a proper noun and like all nouns is typically emitted in conjunction with other words, themselves palpable events which say something about Barbara. Finally, it is ordinarily safe to assume (in the case of proper nouns) that there is a female person in the presence of whom it is appropriate to emit the word "Barbara," and that this observable entity acted in such a manner that her brother was propelled over the rail. But when we announce for the benefit of our listeners that "an expectancy caused the behavior manifested by Barbara," we have another matter. The term "expectancy," whether a written or spoken verbal stimulus, is palpable enough, and like other common nouns can acceptably be uttered in conjunction with predicate terms. The problem is that no one has ever observed the entity or process in the presence of which it is presumably appropriate to emit the word "expectancy." As a consequence, we have seen a variety of so-called operational definitions which typically take the form of self-reports. Subjects are asked, for example, to state the probability that their supervisor will recog-

---

[1]Editor's note: Any resemblance to the name of the editor of this book or editor's brother is purely coincidental.

nize (reinforce) them if they complete an assignment on time. Now it is clear that statements of subjective probability, like other forms of behavior, can be evoked, recorded, added, subtracted and apparently multiplied, but surely no one would claim that the statements *are* the expectancies. Thus, fundamental questions remain: What is the nature of expectancies? Where can they be found? How can they be altered or developed? How do they bring about the behavior we observe? It was this latter question, incidentally, that led Guthrie to complain that Tolman's expectancies seemed to leave the rat lost in thought at the choice point. These questions are by no means trivial. The moral of the story is this: One does not *explain* behavior by attributing it to an expectancy until one also explains the expectancy.

Please note that I am not denying the importance of events taking place beneath the skin. It has been said that we behaviorists are only concerned with the development of input-output relations, and that we treat the organism as a black box. But there is no evidence that we have ever ignored the central nervous system or denied its participation in behavior; for more than 50 years behaviorists have manifested a vital interest in behavioral processes crudely described as feelings, thinking and consciousness. Furthermore, technical advances made every day are showing that the skin, indeed the skull, is not all that important a boundary. Ironically, it has been behaviorists and psychophysiologists, utilizing conditioning methodology, who have told us something about the nature of once-private events and the environmental variables of which they are a function. That is a long and fascinating story which cannot be detailed here, but for the moment let me say that we have *not* found a little man in the central nervous system. Nor have we found an expectancy (big or little) which is more or less insensitive to external events and which, in some fashion, exercises control over operant behavior. What we have found, in most cases, is simply more behavior to be explained, with interesting properties to be sure, but amenable to the same sort of functional analysis as behavior more readily observed.

To provide but one example, we might turn briefly to studies of the reticular formation made possible by the implantation of recording electrodes in that area of the central nervous system. Although these studies are of recent vintage and by no means complete, there are unmistakable indications that reinforcing stimuli *elicit* (cause) respondent activity in the reticular formation. Furthermore, like other classes of respondent behavior (e.g., salivation, heart rate and galvanic skin responses), it now seems apparent that reticular arousal responses can come to be elicited by any neutral stimulus (the conditioned stimulus) that has occurred prior to, or concomitant with, a reinforcing event (the unconditioned stimulus). Unlike other forms of respondent behavior, however, reticular arousal responses seem to condition more rapidly and with a longer interval between the occurrence of the conditioned stimulus and the occurrence of the reinforcing stimulus. Since every operant conditioning treatment provides for the classical pairing of the reinforcing stimulus with other features of the environment in which operant behavior has been reinforced, those and similar features will come to *elicit* reticular arousal responses. But while reticular arousal responses may interact with operant responses in various ways, they cannot possibly serve as causes because they often occur *after* the operant sequence has been initiated. Human beings may report, when asked, that they feel aroused, excited, enthusiastic or that they *expect* to be rewarded, but neither the report itself nor the things presumably reported can be regarded as causes.[1]

To return to the issue at hand, there is no question that organizational leaders alter and/or sustain the behavior of others, and with varying degrees of effectiveness, as I have noted elsewhere (Scott, 1977). Leaders elicit respondent behavior which is typically described, however vaguely, as feeling or emotion. They may also evoke and sustain complex operant behavior, both verbal and nonverbal and covert as well as overt. But our preoccupation with expectancies and other hypothetical constructs in leadership inquiries has not produced useful information about the manner in which leaders may bring about behavioral change. I am not objecting to speculations about events that we cannot see or otherwise observe. In every science, it is recognized, taken for granted, in fact, that it is both necessary and fruitful to talk about things which are, for the moment, unobservable. My principal objection is to the endless postulation of mysterious inner causes which seem to belong to an unknowable, nonphysical world on the one hand, and which are only vaguely related, if at all, to environmental events on the other. They do not, and cannot, provide useful explanations of behavior for aspiring leaders, and worse, they have served to divert our inquiries away from environmental events, which would provide a more satisfactory account.

Martin Evans: It is ironic, I think, that we are having this debate at an Academy of Management meeting. It seems to me

---

[1]This is a good example of a behavioral interpretation of a cognitive concept — we examine those features of *behavior* which have led cognitive theorists to speak of expectancies. It is unlikely, however, that I have satisfied Dr. Evans. Expectancies seem to have an emotional component which beliefs or cognitions do not, and if Evans prefers cognitions over expectancies, he may be implying that his postulated causes of behavior are more rational-intellectual than emotional in nature. If so he would no doubt object to my behavioral interpretation. Perhaps it is the case that while some mentalistic expressions can be translated into behavior, other terms such as expectancy and path instrumentality can be discarded as meaningless or unnecessary (Skinner, 1974, p. 17).

MARTIN G. EVANS

A Professor at the University of Toronto, Martin G. Evans holds his Ph.D. in Administrative Sciences from Yale University. His contributions to current management thought have appeared in the *Journal of Applied Psychology, Studies in Personnel Psychology, Personnel Journal* and *Academy of Management Journal*. He is a member of the Academy of Management, American Psychological Association, American Sociological Association, British Psychological Society, Canadian Association of Administrative Sciences, and Canadian Psychological Association.

He is on the Editorial Board of the *Academy of Management Journal* and serves as an occasional referee for *Journal of Applied Psychology, Canadian Journal of Behavioral Science, Human Relations, European Journal of Social Psychology,* and *European Business.*

Dr. Evans' current research focuses on the path-goal theory of motivation and the impact of motivation on leadership behavior.

that from a reading of the psychological literature it is very clear that the cognitive — oops, acognitive (forgive the Freudian slip) — theories are dead. In many fields of psychology there has been a shift from a behavioristic to a cognitive approach. These include learning theory (Bolles, 1972), motivation (Dember, 1974), verbal condition (Dulany, 1968; Spielberger and DeNike, 1966), systematic desensitization (Lick and Bootzin, 1975; Bandura et al., 1977) and personality theory (Mischel, 1973). I want to look, very selectively, at a couple of these areas and try to link them into the path goal theory of leadership that Bob House and I have been working on over the past few years.

The path goal theory of leadership integrates leader behavior with the expectancy theory of motivation. As such it makes explicit use of unobservable constructs such as expectancies, instrumentalities and valences. This theory is therefore subject to attack by behaviorists. I shall attempt to make a defense of the usefulness of these concepts of predicting behavior in organizations.

The expectancy theory of motivation has been elaborated by Vroom (1964), Campbell, Dunnette, Lawler and Weick (1970) and Wahba and House (1974). In this theory, an individual's overall motivation to behave in a particular way is seen as a function of:

1. The *intrinsic* attractiveness of the behavior.

2. The attraction of *sucessful accomplishment* (task success) coupled with the *expectation* that such sucess follows from putting in effort.

3. The attractiveness of a set of *extrinsic* rewards (pay, promotion, recognition, friendship, status, etc.) coupled with the *expectations* that reward follows success and that success follows effort.

We argue that an important role of the leader is to strengthen the individual's beliefs that his or her effort will lead to effective performance (Effort ⟶ Performance Expectancy) and to strengthen the belief that performance leads to reward (Performance ⟶ Reward Expectancy). It is the motivational contribution of these two expectancies that Scott denies.

Let us look at some examples from a couple of areas of psychology in which the evidence suggests that expectancies (yes, inner events) are vital for the understanding and predicting of behaviors. For the effort ⟶ performance expectancy such evidence exists in the literature on systematic desensitization. For performance ⟶ reward expectation, we shall look at the verbal conditioning literature. These two areas, systematic desensitization and verbal conditioning, are the strongholds of behaviorists, and they cannot very well ignore their own prescriptions.

EFFORT ⟶ PERFORMANCE

Bandura and his associates (1977) argue strongly for the role of "efficacy beliefs" (i.e., the expectancy that putting in effort or trying will lead to accomplishment) as an important mediator in producing behavioral changes. For example, let's look at their studies of the handling of snakes by subjects experiencing severe snake phobia. What Bandura and his associates argue is that the process of social learning (whether through direct experience, vicarious experience or verbal mands) does not affect behavior directly, but rather that social learning builds up the individual's sense of efficacy, his or her belief that it is possible to engage in the behavior. Not surprisingly, they found that this sense of efficacy was strongest for those who had the direct experience of going through a standard program of systematic desensitization, that it was weakest for those who observed subjects going through the program (vicarious experience) and that there was little or no change for those in a control group. The major evidence to support the importance of efficacy beliefs comes from an analysis of post-treatment behavior for that group of subjects who performed at the highest level (i.e., letting a snake roam over their bodies — yeech) during the training phase of the study. Even the individuals who exhibited maximum desensitization still showed variation in their efficacy beliefs, and it is the individual's efficacy beliefs rather than his or her training performance that are the best predictors of performance on later occasions, especially when the individual is asked to generalize his or her behavior to new situations (i.e., dealing with a different species of snake). From the data of this study we can conclude that for generalization of behavior to occur it is essential for the individual to build up a belief that he *can* perform the task. Without this belief, even if the subject has performed tasks of a comparable level of difficulty, he will not maintain the behavior in different situations. This example clearly suggests that the control, prediction and understanding of behavior is enhanced by knowledge of efficacy beliefs, even in the simple application of desensitization procedures in the treatment of phobias.

Applying these results to the more complex area of leadership, I would argue that the leader is an important source of the effort—→performance expectancies of subordinates. In order for a subordinate to have clear and high expectancies that effort leads to performance, the individual needs to know:

1. What is expected in terms of task success, i.e., the standard of performance expected by the organization.
2. What the activities (paths) are that lead to these goals.

3. That he or she has the ability to engage in these activities.

4. Whether or not the activities have resulted in successful task accomplishment.

By providing information on standards, information about required activities and feedback about the outcome of these activities, the leader can start to build up subordinate beliefs about effort and performance. The supervisor can also increase the ability and skill of the subordinate through training, demonstration and coaching. Finally, the supervisor can enhance or destroy the subordinate's knowledge about his or her ability by either showing confidence in the subordinate's ability to perform at a high standard or showing contempt for the subordinate's efforts. Some evidence for this is found in the work of Berlew and Hall (1966) showing that a manager's expectations of a subordinate in an initial job are related to subsequent advancement in the organization by that subordinate. In addition, we can speculate that the model of role-making in vertical dyadic linkages between supervisor and subordinate is triggered by such a mechanism (Dansereau et al., 1975). We should, however, point out that the results reported by these authors do not explicitly evoke the concept of expectancy as a mediating variable between environmental (leader) stimuli and subordinate response. As the authors do not specifically test the intervening relationships, the data are also consistent with a reinforcement paradigm.

It seems to me that one of the tasks for future research is to explore the process and the extent to which the effects found are the result of a subtle continuing reinforcement process (as Scott contends), or whether they are in fact mediated by the individual's awareness of his or her superiors' expectations and hence his or her own sense of efficacy. It is enough, for the purpose of arguing the negative of this resolution, to establish that these expectations may affect behavior through the individual's interpretive processes.

PERFORMANCE→REWARD EXPECTANCIES

The evidence that I draw on to support the existence of these expectancies comes from the areas of verbal conditioning. Most of us are familiar with the series of studies by Dulany (1968), which are described in some detail by Mitchell and Biglan (1971). Dulany found that an individual's behavioral intent and behavior could be predicted from a knowledge of the subject's performance→reward beliefs (Mitchell and Biglan call these instrumentalities), value of rewards, other people's beliefs about how he or she should behave, and desire to conform to these other beliefs. In particular, when the last two components were controlled, variance in the behavior itself was predicted by variance in performance→ reward beliefs and the value of the reward (i.e., the simple expectancy model of motivation). The problem that acognitive theorists raise with these findings is a subtle one (and Scott has, I think, raised it this afternoon). Is the expectancy a precursor and predictor of behavior, or is it merely a correlate of behavior? Spielberger and DeNike (1966) state the issues clearly. There are four possible alternatives that behaviorists might use to explain why performance——→reward beliefs appear to correlate with behavioral change:

1. The possibility that the experimenter or the situation provides the individual with cues that allows him or her to construct an hypothesis about the reward schedule *after* verbal conditioning has taken place.
2. The possibility that after verbal conditioning takes place subjects

notice the performance——→reward contingency and then label this and report the expectancy.

3. Following the process outlined immediately above, subjects who are made aware of the contingency show an additional performance increment. (though this explanation also has a cognitive element).

4. The conditioning process results in the verbalization of the reinforcement principal, as well as in increased performance. I think that this is what Scott means when he says "reinforcing events not only increase the probability of behavior upon which they are made contingent, they elicit . . . responses [which] occur within the skin."

Let us proceed to evaluate these four behavioristic interpretations. The startling findings by Spielberger and DeNike (1966) showed to the contrary that:

A. Performance increments over time occurred for subjects who were *aware* of the contingency hypothesis.

B. Performance increased markedly in the trial at which subjects reported that they became aware of the contingency.

These results and the procedures used by Spielberger and DeNike (1966) rule out the possibility of sensitization to the expectancies (No. 1 above); the labeling hypothesis (No. 2); the hypothesis of a gradual increase during conditioning, followed by a further increase after awareness (No. 3); and the simultaneous conditioning position (No. 4). Thus we can conclude that performance——→ reward beliefs play an important *causal* role in the determination of behavior, that is, precede and affect behavior. Reinforcement alone in the verbal conditioning paradigm is not enough; the reinforcement contingencies must be known by the subjects. Once again, we are drawn to the conclusion that expectancies about performance⟶ reward links play an important role in motivating behavior.

Having established that the cognitive element of performance⟶reward beliefs is important in understanding individual behavior, we should now examine the role of the supervisor in establishing or modifying these beliefs. How can the supervisor play a part in increasing these performance reward links? First, the subordinate needs feedback about whether or not he or she performed effectively. The supervisor is one source of such feedback. To provide accurate feedback to subordinates the supervisor needs (1) to be able to discriminate between effective and ineffective performance; (2) to be able to give feedback that is clear, specific and operational. Secondly, the subordinate must accept the organization's evaluation of his or her performance; when the supervisors allow subordinate participation in goal-setting, the subordinate is likely to accept the latter's evaluation. Thirdly, subordinates must receive valued rewards from the organization that are contingent on performance. The supervisor (1) can communicate the organizational contingencies to subordinates; (2) make consistent recommendations to his or her supervisors for rewards based upon high subordinate performance; and (3) have high upward influence so that his or her recommendations are acted upon and he or she can deliver the promised rewards to subordinates. Fourthly, subordinates must receive personal rewards from the supervisor based upon performance; the supervisor must ensure contingent delivery of his or her rewards of friendship. Finally, subordinates must secure rewards of recognition based upon performance from the work group or from clients of the organization. The leader can encourage the group to set norms of high performance; he or she can insure that subordinates receive the credit from outsiders for work well done rather than take the credit himself or herself.

A number of studies (Oldham, 1976; Reitz, 1971; Sims, 1977) have explored the contingent reward power of the leader to affect subordinate responses. These generally support the proposition that leaders who engage in contingent reward or contingent punishment have more productive and satisfied employees. Sims also found a reciprocal negative effect of performance on contingent reward, suggesting that supervisors were seen to be "stretching the schedule." These studies, however, do not explicitly invoke the notion of expectancy, so they could be explained by either a reinforcement or a cognitive paradigm.

A study that specifically tests the notion of contingency awareness is that of Johnson (1975). In an experimental setting, subjects initially working on a reinforcement schedule that reinforced quantity of work were shifted to a new schedule based upon quality of work. The investigator manipulated two variables; (1) he emphasized (or did not) the importance of doing high quality work; (2) he announced (or did not) that quality rather than quantity would be rewarded (in a third condition there was an unannounced continuation of the quantity reinforcement schedule). He found no differences in quality or quantity of work when groups on the quality reinforcement schedule were compared to those with announced versus unannounced contingencies of reinforcement. However, it does appear that announcement of the contingencies (as cognitive theorists would predict) had a significant impact upon awareness of the contingencies. Unfortunately, Johnson's awareness data are retrospective, so the results could be due to (1) a conditioned response, (2) labelling or (3) differential suggestion. In addition, analyses were not designed to test whether individual performance increased in the trial at which awareness occurred. As a result, this study is equivocal about the role of the leader as the communicator of contingencies. It is clear, however, from other research that stated contingencies, if unsupported by real world contingencies, will rapidly wash out. Extinction is a phenomenon to beware of! The early finding of Pelz (1952), Wager (1965) and House et al. (1971) that upward influence of the supervisor moderates the consideration/satisfaction/performance relationship is congruent with this position. If the leader cannot deliver on (implicit) promises, then the reinforcement contingencies are not met and the hoped for behavior is extinguished.

The moral to my story: There is evidence to suggest that cognitive theories in general, and path goal theory in particular, help us to understand and predict behavior that cannot be explained using reinforcement theories alone. The most important corollary of this statement is that our behaviors, and perceptions, are affected by our own individual expectations about the world. Without knowledge of these expectations — "inner events," as Scott calls them — we cannot hope to develop a science of human behavior. My dog can easily be trained to salivate at the sound of a bell, but it's not going to be so easy to train me. I *expect* to resist.

Bill Scott: Annoucements of the death of behaviorism have appeared once or twice before and are to be regarded more as a form of wishful thinking than anything else. The reinforcement paradigm is alive and quite well, thank you. But so, too, is the cognitive paradigm, or at least it is still kicking, albeit rather feebly.

In a more serious vein, I dare say that, until recently, the cognitive paradigm prevailed in the field of organizational behavior. In fact, it was so dominant that a few years ago in Seattle, I felt moved to point out that there was *another* paradigm, largely ignored in the field and capable of providing a more comprehensive and more parsimonious account of behavior in organizations than the one which then prevailed. I went further to predict that a rapprochement would take place in a few years and that the rapprochement would take the form of a successful integration of the empirical generalizations from the cognitive paradigm within a reinforcement framework. I still maintain that the paradigms will converge and in the manner which I described, but it was obviously foolish to assume that it would only take five years. Meanwhile, we are in the midst of a paradigm conflict.

Paradigm conflicts are not all bad. A more charitable, and possibly more accurate, view is that they are a sign of a vital and maturing field, but they pose some problems. Kuhn (1970), in his discussion of scientific paradigms and scientific revolutions, was wrong, in my judgment, on several counts, but he seems to have been quite correct on one: namely, that proponents of each paradigm attend to, and otherwise respond in the presence of, behavioral phenomena so differently that they talk *through* each other with virtually no impact on each other. You may have already noted that effect, and you will note it now as I ignore Marty's comments and go on to make more of my own. He had no impact on me, you see.

A second problem with the expectancy postulate, and this *is* in response to Marty's comments, is the often tacit assumption that most important classes of behavior occur only after some sort of rational consideration of alternatives. To restate the essence of the expectancy formulation, the individual is postulated to attach different values or utilities to outcomes, then to determine the probability of various outcomes following each of several acts in that setting, then to choose those acts which will maximize the expected value of an outcome and, *finally*, to behave.

Few behaviorists, and none that I know, would disagree with the assertion that human beings sometimes analyze the reinforcement contingencies which surround them, think, solve problems or consider alternatives before behaving otherwise.[1] Our objection is to the proposition that they always do and to the notion that these and other so-called cognitive processes are to be regarded as fundamental *causes* of behavior rather than more behavior to be explained.

Perhaps the most important lesson that can be learned from our examination of the effects of ever more complex environmental treatments is that when human beings engage in activities typically described as "cognitive," they are *behaving,* and that this behavior can come to be understood as a function of environmental events.

It is obvious, of course, that the behavior evoked by various features of a given setting sometimes fails to satisfy the reinforcement contingencies prevailing therein. Unfortunately, the ineffective behavior may persist, or there may be oscillation from one ineffective form to another. Emotional responses elicited by the occurrence of aversive reinforcers or the continued absence of positive reinforcers may also intrude, further precluding the appearance of more effective operants. (In the vernacular, we may say that the individual is "frustrated," in a "state of conflict" or "depressed.") If, however, we have been fortunate enough to have been exposed to the appropriate social reinforcement contingencies, we are quite likely to "stop and think" or engage in other types of problem-solving behavior. We do not literally stop

---

[1] It is for this reason that I find Marty's Freudian slip so intriguing. Could it be that his growing familiarity with the reinforcement paradigm has led him to "subconsciously re-*cognize*" that behaviorists have told us more about cognitive processes than cognitivists?[2]

[2] *Editor's note:* Cognitivists? Good grief!

behaving, of course. Nor is it true that our subsequent, and possibly more effective, behavior then comes under the control of some mysterious process located in the mind. Rather, what happens is that some features (stimulus events) in the setting evoke various forms of precurrent or self-controlling operant responses which, by generating *additional* discriminative stimuli (S_D's), increase the probability that an effective operant will occur. If, in fact, the problem-solving operants produce additional S_D's which evoke behavior which satisfies the prevailing contingencies (the solution operant), then the resulting stimulus consequences will reinforce both the solution operant *and* the problem-solving operants as well.

One straightforward example of a problem-solving operant is the act of asking another person to tell one how to behave. New employees may not often emit this problem-solving operant, because others (including the supervisor) may punish them when it is revealed that effective behavior is lacking. If that contingency does not prevail, however, and the question is asked, the supervisor or another employee may provide an S_D in the form of a verbal description of the reinforcement contingency (i.e., a description of the behavior required, the circumstances under which the behavior should be emitted and possibly the reinforcing consequences). If the description provided by another evokes an operant similar to that which set the occasion for the provider's description and if the description is accurate, effective behavior may then occur. I should note that I have described a form of stimulus control which is a fundamental process in operant conditioning. Stimulus control refers to the empirical observation that when an operant response is reinforced in the presence of a stimulus event, that stimulus (the S_D) will come to *evoke* the operant when it is presented or naturally occurs. (The term "evoke" refers to the observation that the S_D increases the probability that the operant will occur, though the probability is not often 1.00 as in *elicitation.*) Propositional control, the form of stimulus control I just alluded to, refers to the observation that verbal stimuli in the form of verbs (whether spoken or written), rules, maxims or propositions often serve as S_D's in human behavior, because we are reinforced for behaving in specified ways in their presence.

Another example of a rather simple kind of problem-solving operant is the act of observing or attending to specific features of the setting. A new employee in an organizational setting might "survey the scene" or look more closely at a stimulus configuration and, in doing so, may generate S_D's which evoke effective operants. For example, a written description of the manner in which the equipment is to be operated may be discovered and read. The solution operant of operating the equipment is then evoked by the S_D's which the problem-solving operant generated.

Of all the stimulus events to be observed in an organizational setting, the behavior of other incumbents is of special significance. Thus, if effective solution operants are not immediately available or the new incumbent has behaved ineffectively, he or she may turn and observe the manner in which others are behaving and possibly the reinforcing consequences. The problem-solving operant of turning and observing the behavior of others thus produces an S_D which evokes imitative operants.

Individuals may also observe *their own behavior* and its consequences and thereby produce S_D's evoking more effective task responses. Observed operants which are not followed by reinforcers serve as S_Δs (marked as errors) and are not repeated, while those which are followed by reinforcing events serve as S_D's, evoking more behavior of the same topography.

In all the above examples, additional and quite important problem-solving operants may occur. If, for example, the verbal instructions provided by another are complex or the instrumental solution response must be delayed, the individual may "rehearse" the instructions. Later, when the solution operant sequence is required, the individual may then repeat the instructions, thus reinstating the S_D which serves to evoke the instrumental responses. In the same manner, the individual who solves the problem by attending to the behavior of others in that setting may also respond verbally by describing the behavior of others and its reinforcing consequences. The description, when later repeated by the problem solver, serves as the S_D evoking the instrumental behavior which he or she earlier observed. Finally, individuals who have been conditioned to do so may not only observe their own behavior but also describe it as it occurs. Running commentaries of this sort, even if only fragmentary or tentative (hypotheses), will often serve to eliminate ineffective behavior (as when the individual says to himself, "Nothing happened when I pressed the lever when the light was yellow") and speed the appearance of effective instrumental responses (as when the individual says, "Possibly the experimenter will give me points if I press the lever only when the light is green").

The additional problem-solving operants I have just described may occur in overt form. The individual may talk out loud, and both the operant responses and the auditory stimulation which they produce may be readily observed by another. But verbal behavior, like other classes of operants, can easily occur on such a reduced scale that it cannot be detected by others. Furthermore, it may remain at the "covert" level when the speaker is also the listener, for in speaking to oneself, it is typically more effective and much easier *not* to talk out loud.

Covert problem-solving behavior is unquestionably fascinating if only because it seems so mysterious. It is frequently inaccessible to another observer and may often go undetected by the problem solver himself. It is only rarely identical in form to its overt counterpart, and the same musculature is not involved. The fact that it is often covert and, when effective, produces S_D's evoking behavior that is more easily observed has no doubt been responsible for the postulation of expectancies, cognitions, "aware-nesses"[1] and other mentalistic causes. But covert reponses are not the cause of overt responses, nor does covert behavior have mystical or nonphysical properties. It is usually acquired in overt form and can easily be shaped or taught at that level. Furthermore, covert behavior, verbal or otherwise[2], can easily revert to the overt form. When, for example, covert problem-solving operants fail to produce S_D's which effectively evoke instrumental solution responses, individuals quickly begin to talk out loud to themselves, draw sketches of the objects or events, or write

[1] I had not planned to discuss the concept of "awareness," but since Dr. Evans has raised the issue, I should point out that the analysis by Spielberger and DeNike, to which he refers, appears in a book by Larry Cummings and myself (Scott and Cummings, 1973). In my judgement, their analysis is quite useful in revealing to the student (1) that there are competing paradigms in our field, (2) that behaviorists have not ignored the behavioral processes broadly implied by the term "awareness," and (3) the inevitable confusion produced by the introduction of "nomological networks." Otherwise, few if any conclusions can be drawn from the studies they describe, and certainly *not* the conclusion that instrumental task responses (performance gains) are caused by an internal cognitive state or process called awareness.

[2] It would be a mistake to assume that all covert problem-solving operants are "verbal." Individuals can be taught to observe objects and events so that the behavior of seeing them again can occur in the absence of the objects and events seen. Operant seeing can be evoked by the presentation of appropriate S_D's, as may be demonstrated when I ask you to "imagine the front door of your dwelling place." But we also can be conditioned to behave so as to produce S_D's which evoke operant seeing in ourselves. In a problem setting, for example, we may stimulate ourselves so as to see again the behavior of others, though they are neither present nor behaving, and in doing so, we may effectively evoke that behavior in its overt forms. In all such cases, we are not conjuring up a copy or some sort of internal representation of the things seen. Rather, we are evoking behavior similar to that which occurred when the things were present.

down the instruction. In these cases, the problem-solving operants *and* the S_D's which are produced are readily observed by others.[1]

The appearance of operant behavior which satisfies the contingencies prevailing in a given setting does *not* mean that precurrent problem-solving operants have inevitably occurred. The setting may be similar, if not identical, to those to which the individual had been previously exposed. In those cases, effective solution operants appear so quickly that there is simply no time for precurrent problem-solving operants to occur. Moreover, if we always engaged in behavior characterized as attending, thinking, reasoning or imagining before behaving otherwise in some hazardous settings, we would be quite dead.

Thinking or problem-solving operants are most likely to occur when the setting is novel or one in which the reinforcement contingencies are unusual, changing or otherwise complex (as in laboratory studies of "problem solving"). If they are effective in producing S_D's which evoke solution operants, we should not be surprised to see the latter appear suddenly and at full strength. Then the problem-solving operants fade or extinguish because they are unnecessary and quite probably dysfunctional. For example, the adolescent learning to drive may ask the trainer what to do and then try to respond appropriately upon instructions; or, alternatively, after observing an effective driver and/or covertly describing effective behavior, the driver may later "imagine" or describe to himself the behavior earlier observed, thus evoking effective driving

---

[1]In presenting this operant analysis of thinking and problem solving, I may well have provided a "reinforcement interpretation" of another mentalistic expression—in this case, a cognition or cognitive process. If so, it may be more to the liking of Dr. Evans, who apparently wishes to distinguish between rationalintellectual inner causes and those which have an emotional component. It should be obvious, however, that I have not turned cognitive. Nor have I unduly stretched an operant formulation to meet the criticism that reinforcement theorists have "beheaded" the organism. The basic features of my analysis of thinking and problem solving were introduced over a quarter of a century ago (Skinner, 1953).

operants. You can well "imagine" the consequences of failing to bring the car to a stop if problem-solving operants inevitably preceded each stop.

Problem-solving operants are not guaranteed even in unusual settings. Human beings and other organisms, become active in novel settings. They do so, in part, because, as we now know, novel stimuli *elicit* reticular arousal responses. (The Russians call them orienting responses or "animation" reflexes.) In some cases, at least, effective solution operants are gradually shaped from these undifferentiated behavioral units by a procedure which, when systematically applied, is called the method of successive approximations. It is difficult to rule out the occurrence of problem-solving operants in this case, for as I have indicated, they are often covert. However, we have some indication that they do not occur when effective solution operants only *gradually* emerge. (Solution operants typically appear at full strength when problem-solving operants have preceded them.) More direct evidence of the occurrence or non occurrence of problem-solving operants will become available as we continue to study this class of behavior, for as Skinner (1953, p. 282) has noted, the line between covert and overt behavior shifts with the development of every new technique for making private events public.

Martin Evans: Bill's comment about the rat reminds me of a story written by Bertrand Russell in which the rats seemed to take on the characteristics of their investigators. For example, in American labs the rats run around very actively, rush through the maze and eventually find their goals through a long series of trials and errors; Germanic rats, however, sit and cogitate, think, and finally make the rational choice. It seems that Bill and I are those two rats. I leave it to you to decide which is which.

There's one point that I want to make very strongly. It's clear that, as Ed Locke was saying, stimuli are not just out there. It's our interpretation of those stimuli, our beliefs and our expectancies that cause us to behave. No one is denying that those expectations and those beliefs are based upon reality. No one is denying that environmental stimuli *are* a source of these expectancies. I've observed the world, I've observed the contingencies, and I created my beliefs around that. But it is my interpretation, *not* the buzzing confusion out there, that results in my behavior.

Bill Scott argues that cognitive behavior, i.e., computing expectancies, judging anticipated satisfaction and choosing behaviors, is just one more form of behavior to be explained in behavioristic terms.

If this is the case, he needs to show us the conditions under which these behaviors occur and the conditions under which they do not occur. Further, and I think this is the problem, he has to show how individuals make choices between behaviors; presumably these choices require some calculation of obtainable utilities!

I guess one research issue that's not totally centered around leadership but relates to leadership motivation is the question: What kinds of cognitions do we build up that are associated with different reinforcement schedules? Is it that I believe the reward will come once every two times, or if I do two things I will get a reward? Those are two different kinds of cognition whose implications could and should be explored empirically if we are to make maximum use of both cognitive and reinforcement paradigms.

Bill Scott: I repeat that the behaviorist's objection is *not* that human beings do not think, solve problems or consider behavior-outcome relations. On the contrary, they sometimes do and often with important reinforcing advantages. I agree that thinking, problem solving and quite possibly expectancies or path goal instrumentalities *can* come to be understood, not as mystical inner causes, but as more behavior, made of "real stuff" and subject to the same sorts of environmental events as other classes of behavior. We *will* come to understand it in the sense of being able to predict, evoke and (most importantly) *develop more effective forms of it.* We will be able to do so if, and only if, we continue to examine its properties and the environmental variables of which it is a function. It has not been, nor will it become, an easy chore, for behaviors are complex, often fleeting, and sometimes covert. Even so, progress has been made, and cognitive theorists have obviously contributed to our knowledge of the structure of that behavior. But they have confused their constituents and themselves by holding up these activities as causes rather than as more behavior to be explained, and they have provided us with little information about the environmental circumstances responsible for that behavior.

In the brief time remaining, I should like, first, to provide a word of caution. It has been claimed that proponents of the cognitive and reinforcement paradigms are really saying the same thing. We are not. We are, to be sure, observing and attempting to comprehend the same phenomenon — human behavior in all its complexity — but we are decidedly not saying the same things about it. If we were, we would be emitting the same words or possibly different words with the same meaning. We are doing neither. When cognitive theorists utter the words "expectancy," "intention," or "path goal instrumentality," they are referring to internal events, not directly observed, which are believed to cause or produce complex sequences of behavior which *are* observed. If behaviorists utter such words, they are referring, however obliquely, to classes of behavior which, though frequently difficult to detect, are, in principle, observable and which are hypothesized and increasingly found to be a function of *environmental* events. These are important differences, the ramifications of which may escape your attention if you are inclined to dismiss the debate as a series of empty verbalisms designed for the sole purpose of entertaining the audience.

Finally, if I may be so presumptuous, a word of advice for the younger generation of scientists, for it is they who will achieve the much needed rapprochement. I urge you to examine the reinforcement paradigm, not as cognitive theorists have interpreted it, but as it really is. And when you do, I believe you will come to enjoy its advantages in your studies of leadership. I think we all agree that effective leaders are those who evoke, shape and/or sustain the desired behavior of others. And they do so by altering the only events over which they have some access and control: the various features of the environment in which the behavior of others takes place. The reinforcement paradigm encourages us to look there in the first place, to observe carefully those features of the world which an effective leader alters, and to observe and classify the leader behaviors which produce those alterations.

But it is also the case that the two paradigms make contact at several points, and for that reason it would be perilous to ignore the cognitive paradigm. After all, cognitive theorists conduct research once in a while, and when they employ experimental strategies, as contrasted with systematic assessment approaches, they introduce environmental changes and observe consequent behavioral outcomes. We may admit that the experimental treatments provided by cognitive researchers often contain complex instructions, the significance of which they sometimes overlook, but instructions *are* environmental events just as surely as warning lights, changes in the sound of equipment and increases in pay.

Martin Evans: Some of the speakers on the other side of the debate (with the exception of Bill Scott) have talked as if they have the corner on science, as if they were scientists and the rest of us weren't. I react strongly and negatively to that stimulus! Even so, there are some things we can learn from the acognitive paradigm that will help us refine cognitive models:

BE SPECIFIC ABOUT BEHAVIOR

What behaviors do you want subordinates to engage in? What behaviors does the leader engage in? As a corollary, the question of measuring these behaviors becomes vital. Too many of our scales for measuring leadership are cluttered with excess baggage. We have to be clear conceptually about what we want to measure and then be sure that we measure just that and nothing more. We are guilty of two principal sins:

1. We slop in excess conceptual meaning to operational definitions of our constructs. For example, both House (1971) and I (Evans, 1970) argue that the original LBDQ (Fleishman et al., 1955) consideration scales measure empathy, i.e., the extent to which the supervisor is *aware of* the different needs of subordinates. The scale, of course, actually measures the supervisor's *concern* for the needs of subordinates; awareness implies the existence of diagnostic and communication skills that are not tapped by the scale.

2. The operational measure of a particular concept in fact taps several different constructs. The original LBDQ initiation scale has items which tap both setting standards, pushing for production, and also punitive and authoritarian behavior by the superior.

The lesson is to (1) identify the different kinds of leader behavior — in Scott's terms, a topography; (2) develop ways of measuring or observing these different behaviors; and (3) (and here I part company with our behaviorist colleagues) develop a nomological network of relationships that link these observed and inferred leader behaviors to observable and unobservable outcomes.

CLARIFY ASSUMPTIONS

The use of the reinforcement paradigm forces us to be very clear about our assumptions and about auxiliary hypotheses (cf. Mahwinney and Ford's [1977] treatment of House's path-goal hypothesis — the effect of leader path-goal clarification when the task is ambiguous assumes that followers have *lower* path-goal beliefs than may actually be the case).

These benefits of the acognitive paradigm notwithstanding, it is in the lack of basic understanding which comes from the development of a nomological net that our behavioristic colleagues are impoverished. The use of hypothetical constructs helps us to explain and understand rather than merely to predict. I would argue for example, that prior to 1970 the leadership literature was rather inconclusive in its predictions. In that year my introduction of the notions of individual motivation as an intervening variable between leader behavior and subordinate satisfaction and performance provided a basis for reaching a richer understanding of that literature. I did not provide that understanding, but a year later House's contingency path-goal theory advanced our comprehension and understanding of a previously undigested mass of studies. Thus, in terms of theory building and understanding, these concepts, even if they are insufficient and unobservable, have provided useful way stations in the development of a theory.

I regret that I do not see the acognitive approach theories assisting us in achieving a real understanding of leader behavior, or behavior in general. Who remembers Adams and Romney's (1959) "functional analysis of authority"? The role of the acognitive approach seems (both in motivation theory and leadership theory) one of providing a "reinforcement interpretation" of whatever theory we are discussing. It seems, then, that these interpretations are providing a parsimonious restatement of existing theories, and it is a useful contribution. However, I do not believe that the reinforcement approach would have enabled us to develop true theoretical positions. Cognitive theorists lead, behaviorists follow.

REFERENCES AND RECOMMENDED READINGS (Scott)

Evans, M. G. The effects of supervisory behavior upon worker perception of their path-goal relationships. Doctoral dissertation, Yale University, 1968.

House, R. J. A path-goal theory of leader effectiveness. *Administrative Science Quarterly*, 1971, *16*, 321-338.

Kuhn, T. S. *The Structure of Scientific Resolutions*, 2nd Ed. Chicago: University of Chicago Press, 1970.

Scott, W. E., Jr. Leadership: A functional analysis, in J. G. Hunt and L. L. Larson (Eds.): *Leadership: The Cutting Edge.* Carbondale, Ill.: Southern Illinois University Press, 1977.

Scott, W. E., Jr. and Cummings, L. L. *Readings in Organizational Behavior and Human Performance*, Rev. Ed. Homewood, Ill.: Richard D. Irwin, Inc., 1973.

Skinner, B. F. *Science and Human Behavior.* New York: The Free Press, 1953.

Skinner, B. F. *Verbal Behavior.* New York: Appleton-Century-Crofts, 1957.

Skinner, B. F. *About Behaviorism.* New York: Alfred A. Knop, 1974.

Vroom, Victor A. *Work and Motivation.* New York: John Wiley & Sons, 1964.

REFERENCES AND RECOMMENDED READINGS (Evans)

Adams, J. S. and Romney, A. K. A functional analysis of authority. *Psychological Review*, 1959, *56*, 234-251.

Bandura, A., Adams, N.E. and Beyer, J. Cognitive processes mediating behavioral change. *Journal of Personality and Social Psychology*, 1977, *35*, 125-139.

Berlew, D. E. and Hall, D. T. The socialization of managers: Effects of expectations on performance. *Administrative Science Quarterly*, 1966, *11*, 207-223.

Bolles, R. C. Reinforcement, expectancy, and learning. *Psychological Review*, 1972, *79*, 394-409.

Campbell, J. P., Dunnette, M. D., Lawler, E. E. and Weick, K. E. *Managerial Behavior, Performance, and Effectiveness*. New York: McGraw-Hill, 1970.

Dansereau, F., Graen, G. and Haga, W. J. A vertical dyadic linkage approach to leadership within formal organizations: A longitudinal investigation of the role making process. *Organizational Behavior and Human Performance*, 1975, *13*, 46-78.

Dember, W. N. Motivation and the cognitive revolution. *American Psychologist*, 1974, *29*, 161-168.

Dulany, D. E. Awareness, rules, and propositional control: A confrontation with S-R behavior theory, in D. Horton and T. Dixon: *Verbal Behavior and General Behavior Theory*. Englewood Cliffs, N.J.: Prentice-Hall, 1968.

Evans, M. G. The effects of supervisory behavior on the path-goal relationship. *Organizational Behavior and Human Performance*, 1970, *5*, 277-298.

Fleishman, E. A., Harris, E. F. and Burtt, H. E. *Leadership and Supervision in Industry*. Columbus, Ohio: Bureau of Educational Research, 1955.

House, R. J. A path-goal theory of leader effectiveness. *Administrative Science Quarterly*, 1971, *16*, 321-338.

House, R. J., Filley, A. C. and Gujarati, D. N. Leadership style, hierarchical influence and the satisfaction of subordinate role expectations: A test of Likert's influence proposition. *Journal of Applied Psychology*, 1971, *55*, 422-432.

Johnson, G. A. The relative efficacy of stimulus versus reinforcement control for obtaining stable performance change. *Organizational Behavior and Human Performance*, 1975, *14*, 321-341.

Lick, J. and Bootzin, R. Expectancy factors in the treatment of fear: Methodological and theoretical issues. *Psychological Bulletin*, 1975, *82*, 917-931.

Mawhinney, T. C. and Ford, J. D. The path-goal theory of leadership effectiveness: An operant interpretation. *Academy of Management Review*, 1977, *2*, 398-411.

Mischel, W. Toward a cognitive social learning reconceptualization of personality. *Psychological Review*, 1973, *80*, 252-283.

Mitchell, T. R. and Biglan, A. Instrumentality theories: Current uses in psychology. *Psychological Bulletin*, 1971, *76*, 432-454.

Oldham, G. The motivational strategies used by supervisors: Relationship to effectiveness indicators. *Organizational Behavior and Human Performance*, 1976, *15*, 66-86.

Pelz, D. C. Influence: A key to effective leadership in the first line supervisor. *Personnel*, 209-221.

Reitz, H. J. Managerial attitudes and perceived contingencies between performance and organizational response. *Academy of Management Proceedings*, 31st Annual Meeting, 1971, 227-238.

Sims, H. P. The leader as a manager of reinforcement contingencies: An empirical example and a model, in J. G. Hunt and L. L. Larson (Eds.): *Leadership: The Cutting Edge*. Carbondale, Ill.: Southern Illinois University Press, 1977.

Spielberger, C. D., and DeNike, L. D. Descriptive behaviorism versus cognitive theory in verbal operant conditioning. *Psychological Review*, 1966, *73*, 306-325.

Vroom, V. H. *Work and Motivation*. New York, John Wiley & Sons, 1964.

Wager, W. C. Leadership style, influence, and supervisory role obligations. *Administrative Science Quarterly*, 1965, *9*, 391-420.

Wahba, M. and House, R. J. Expectancy theory of work and motivation: Logical and methodological issues. *Human Relations*, 1974, *27*, 121-147.

Part III

CONCLUSION

CHAPTER 7   Comments by the Discussant
CHAPTER 8   Summary and Recommendations
Glossary of Words and Phrases

COMMENTS BY THE DISCUSSANT

Steven Kerr earned his Ph.D. in management from the City University of New York. He is now Professor of Management at the University of Southern California. Prior to joining the faculty there, he spent eight years in industry and seven years on the faculty of the Ohio State University.

Professor Kerr is the coauthor of *Managerial Process and Organizational Behavior* (Scott, Foresman, 1976) and has also authored or coauthored more than 30 articles in academic journals. He is Consulting Editor in Management to Grid Publishing Company, Associate Editor of the *Journal of Business Research*, and a member of the editorial boards of the *Academy of Management Journal* and the Southern Illinois University Leadership Symposium. He is an active member of the Academy of Management, serving frequently in administrative roles and as a presenter and discussant at professional meetings.

STEVEN KERR

I shall attempt to organize this discussion by posing a series of questions. I'm not certain whether these questions can be or even need to be answered, but they may help us to gain a fresh perspective on some of the things the debaters have been talking about.

WHAT ARE THE ETHICAL IMPLICATIONS?

Several speakers asked that we consider the ethical implications of the theories and strategies espoused in these debates. Probably most forceful was Hamner's statement that, while the job is the manager's business, the employee's mind is not. It is doubtful that many of us would argue with this position, but its operationalization is damnably difficult. I personally hesitate to respond to the occasional student complaint that OB teaches how to manipulate people, because I find it increasingly hard to distinguish between manipulation and the important responsibilities of management. In the old days we could take refuge in the argument that, since our prescriptions were inane and our techniques inept, we could no more be accused of messing up employees' minds than we could of getting them to be more effective. But for all our limitations and deficiencies, the odd thing is that today's research suggests that some of the things we try actually work! As a consequence, the ethical question assumes real importance. Nevertheless, I must agree with Locke that it is unrealistic to differentiate changing the job situation from changing the employee's mind. As he pointed out: "Such a dichotomy is illusory. If changing the job situation does *not* change the employee's mind (e.g., goals, knowledge, expectations), then the job change will not work."

In short, we must ask if it is possible to *avoid* messing with people's minds and still make use of the tools of modern management? If it is not, are we confronted with a choice between ethics and efficacy?

HOW IMPORTANT IS PARSIMONY?

Most of us have learned somewhere along the line that one requirement of a sound theory is that it should be parsimonious, but of course the other side of that coin is that it must not be *too* parsimonious, that is, it must not exlude elements which are important for understanding and prediction. The problem here is that it is not possible to study all the phenomena in the world, yet no scientific basis exists for an a priori exclusion of variables. Even variables whose inclusion cannot be justified conceptually may possess such predictive power that their exclusion from a particular model is indefensible. Therefore, it is all well and good to point out, as does Hamner, that most researchers err in their failure to design research to test competing hypotheses. This is a fair and an important criticism, but the fact is that *all* competing hypotheses cannot be tested. In the absence of scientific bases for including some hypotheses and excluding others, the researcher is necessarily left to rely on intuition. Locke's intuition tells him that it is unnecessary to test competing behavioral hypotheses. Hamner faults Locke for this omission, but does not fault him for failing to test the influence upon performance of the shape of subjects' skulls — though in decades past this omission would have been deemed inexcusable.

However we determine what is important to study, we must not become so obsessed with tidiness that we refuse to consider what we cannot see, and decline to measure phenomena merely because their measurement is difficult. Do you remember the joke about the professor who drops a quarter in the middle of a dark street, then looks for it at the corner because there is a lamp post overhead? My own research on organizational reward systems has convinced me that an important failing of many systems is that aspects of worker behavior which are easy to measure are overattended (such as lateness), while critical aspects of behavior go unrewarded because their measurement is difficult. One implication of this for these debates is that we should not decide a priori to focus only on observable behavior, though such a decision might be correct for some purposes. The exclusive use of functional analysis cannot be defended on scientific grounds; it is *not* scientific to be incomplete. It is certainly true that a map of reality must not contain every boulder and pothole in reality, lest it be as difficult to negotiate as reality itself. However, it is equally important that our maps, models and measuring devices not be too simplistic.

If parsimony is your bag and you're also into microtheory, you might be interested to know that, according to Descartes, all behavior is a function of the level of activity of the pineal gland. If you prefer macrotheory I can offer you primitive activism: there are good spirits and bad spirits, you see, and they interact within us to cause us to behave. In Flip Wilsonian terms, the Devil makes us do it. Now such theories are very parsimonious, and they have the further advantage of being untestable! This is no small asset. Nothing is quite so neat, compact and parsimonious as a tautology.

The point is that it has been said of reinforcement (operant) theory that it is tautological. As pointed out by Luthans, "the antecedent only serves to cue the behavior; the behavior still depends on its consequences." It is highly parsimonious to maintain that if you offer someone a reinforcer you get a certain reaction, and it is not necessary to consider mediating processes. Furthermore, if you do not obtain the desired response, then either you have failed to offer a reinforcer (your error) or the subject has failed to correctly perceive the contingencies (his/her error). In no case can it be the theory's error. Yet Ruston (1978) has observed that "a theory which cannot be mortally endangered cannot be alive." So how important is parsimony?

ARE THE WEAKNESSES YOU HEARD DESCRIBED (A) FATAL TO AND (B) INHERENT IN THE THEORIES, MODELS AND PARADIGMS WHICH WERE DISCUSSED?

Since most objections raised by the speakers to each other's positions were pretty persuasive and quite severe, an affirmative response to this question might suggest that we have little left to work toward. However, it seems to me that many of the deficiencies cited are addressable, and the rest can be lived with. For example, it is demonstrably true that most people have very limited ability to calculate expectancies, and it is also the case that most of us have great difficulty in working out contingencies of reinforcement. Does this mean, though, that approaches which depend upon expectancies and reinforcement schedules are doomed? Certainly it is true, as Cummings pointed out, that most of the data offered as evidence of the moderating effects of individual differences are unimpressive. Does this mean that such effects can be dismissed as unimportant? The evidence is equally unimpressive in support of almost all other variables in the social sciences. If we adopted such a stringent criterion, we would dismiss just about everything we do, and therefore ourselves as well. Scott reminds us that we have never seen an expectancy, and Luthans challenges us to show him a leadership or a motivation. Such criticisms may be warranted, but do they deal a death blow to cognitive inquiry?

Not only is it true that the variables we study cannot be shown to be important, it is also true that our methods of inquiry are so poor that whatever conclusions we reach are likely to be artifacts of our design or our measurements. It could even be argued that the higher the observed relationship, the more likely it is that faulty instrumentation or inadequate intervention has caused it. But even assuming that this is true, these are not inherent defects of the various theories and models, but rather problems which need to be and can be addressed in future theory-building and research. I would therefore conclude that, while impressive arguments have been made which pinpoint the weaknesses of the paradigms and models our debators have been discussing, these are neither inherent nor fatal.

WHATEVER HAPPENED TO CONTINGENCIES?

"Man has no mind" is a risky assertion, as Locke pointed out. If you believe that, how do you account for actions which have not been reinforced in the past, and which we know very well will not be reinforced in the future? How do you account for such actions nontautologically, that is, without resorting to such all-purpose cop-outs as self-reinforcement? On the other hand, there's an interesting moment in *The Cactus Flower* when Walter Matthau is caught in a web of inconsistent behaviors and is asked if he has changed his mind. He replies, in a voice filled with self-disgust, "I have no mind, so far as I can tell." To assume that all people have (functioning) minds seems, in light of the behavior we see happening around us, an equally risky assertion.

The point is that, in keeping with the spirit of these debates, most of our debators have offered us a choice of rather extreme, noncontingent "truths" about the universe. For example, we have been presented the argument that cognitions do not influence behaviors but rather are discovered from one's behaviors. It follows that to change the cognition, we must first change the behavior (this logic was offered as the rationale underlying efforts by the Supreme Court to desegregate the South during the Eisenhower administration.) The opposite position — that our cognitions fully determine our behaviors — has also been suggested, and a number of "self-help" books (such as Korda's *Power* and Ringer's *Looking Out For #1*) have made a buck by peddling this assumption as guaranteed truth. As universal statements, however, both are extreme. It is far more sensible to conclude that both cognitions and the environment are necessary (but insufficient alone) to explain behavior.

So whatever happened to contingencies? Is anything always a "best approach" or a "best theory"? Is functional analysis *always* an effective technique? Never effective? Do individual differences never make a difference? Do they always? (There's a bubble-testing job on some automotive assembly lines — checking brake tubes for leaks — that is so boring, fatiguing and eye-straining that virtually nobody will do it. Many equally unpopular jobs could be mentioned.) Do mental processes always guide action? Do they never guide action? Where are the contingencies?

Actually, our debaters are far less extreme than their assigned positions might indicate. Hamner has warned the reader not to accept blindly any of the extreme arguments offered in these debates, and Smith has warned that we must not handicap ourselves by employing tunnel vision about what constitutes "scientific" research. As she points out, we must avail ourselves of *all* available evidence. This should include not only data about theories and positions different from our own but also data which fail to support a position we believe in. Lawler's remark concerning the reluctance of journals to publish statistically insignificant findings is pertinent in this regard, but it would be wrong to lay all the blame upon the journal editors. My own survey of advisory board members of 19 social science journals — 300 respondents altogether — revealed that even competent analyses on timely and important subjects are likely to be rejected if results are not statistically significant (Kerr, Tolliver and Petree, 1977). Through this kind of tunnel vision we disregard much that is valuable and permit unsound theories, models and intervention techniques to acquire successful track records in the research literature.

If advocacy of extreme positions is to be avoided, why hold and now publish these debates? The rationale is Hegelian. Our hope is that by confronting each thesis with its logical opposite (antithesis) a new position (synthesis) may emerge, which contains the best features of each.

WHAT ARE THE COSTS?

First, what are the costs of adopting position A in any debate or position B? For example, if we decide to ignore the influences of cognitive processes upon behavior, or the moderating effects of indivdual differences, what are the costs? One possible cost is that we will get prediction without much explanation. Ideally our theories should explain as well as predict. A further cost is that we are likely to lose predictive power *in those situations or for those people* whose behavior is influenced by the variables we choose to ignore.

Alternatively, what are the costs of insisting upon a determining role for mediating processes of the mind? One might be that we will construct hypothetical processes which cannot be operationalized, cannot be tested, cannot be shown to influence behavior. A related cost is that we may allow our hopes and our values and our assumed truths about Man to turn us toward religion and away from science.

As a third possibility, what are the costs of simultaneously granting provisional acceptance of both sets of beliefs espoused in each debate? Why shouldn't we recognize that in some situations functional analysis is an excellent device, while in others it is inferior to available alternatives? Why shouldn't we accept the fact that some people's behavior cannot be predicted from any knowledge we have or they profess to have about their patterns of reinforcement, while recognizing that other people are predictable as hell? What are the costs of refusing to permit a pedagogical device—these debates—to polarize us? As has already been mentioned, the polarization you have witnessed is largely the result of role prescriptions and task assignments. For example, both Clay Hamner and Bill Scott are actually *enraptured* by cognitive processes, because they know that past reinforcement patterns are inevitably modified by such processes. (What does getting an A on a term paper do to the probability that you will submit the same paper to the same instructor in the future?) Furthermore, Ed Locke and Martin Evans have the *highest* regard for operant approaches, because they know that expectations are in large part a function of one's perceptions about past reinforcement patterns, or information from others about success or failure as they undertook various actions (And Fred Luthans is studying us right now, using a nonfunctional approach!)

In short, what is the harm in keeping *all* of the ideas you have heard during these debates, and even all of the debaters, around for a while longer, at least until we can determine with certainty which set of four we should discard?

REFERENCES AND RECOMMENDED READINGS

Kerr, S., Tolliver, J. and Petree, D. Manuscript characteristics which influcence acceptance for management and social science journals. *Academy of Management Journal*, 1977, *20*, 32-141.

Ruston, W.A.H. Personal communication. Referenced in R. J. House and K.D. MacKenize: Paradigm development in the social sciences: a proposed research strategy. *Academy of Management Review*, 1978, *3* 7-23.

Chapter 8

SUMMARY AND RECOMMENDATIONS

In the last chapter, Steve Kerr suggested that we keep the ideas expressed in this book, and all the debaters, around for a while longer. As your editor, I concur — and then some. Why not use these collected ideas to achieve a better understanding of the world in which we live and work? Why not let contradictory ideas generate a healthy tension, out of which can come productive consequences? For example, some of the scientific "sins" to which our debaters have referred might have been remedied or avoided if the research investigator had kept an open mind. An open mind is more likely to examine alternative hypotheses or competing explanations of results. Open-minded, informed investigators are prepared intellectually and emotionally to consider the possibility that both operant and cognitive models are useful in understanding research data and behavior, whereas errors of interpretation and biases in design are the probable result of wearing theoretical blinders, of limiting one's view of behavior to either operant or cognitive models.

But is the need to be open-minded and informed about different theoretical models limited to those persons who conduct formal research studies? By no means! What about the manager who must allocate resources (spend real money) to cure a motivation or productivity problem? Would it be reasonable to establish a reinforcement program because in general "it works"? Or would it be better to embark on a program to change employees' perceptions and attitudes about the company in general? Would it matter whether the manager is dealing with a motivational problem among chemists or clerks? Engineers or sales personnel? Hairdressers or executives? Yes, it matters. Many other group, individual and organizational factors matter as well. Where specific behavioral goals can be identified, where an historical pattern of behavior can be traced, where performance feedback has been lacking, where sufficient skills are known to exist, under these conditions an operant model may be useful. If, on the other hand, the desired behaviors are complex and unspecified, the situation is novel or the employee new to it, and performance is difficult to measure or feedback to provide, a cognitive model may be preferable.

Better yet, in most job situations these simple and complex conditions coexist, so both models will have potential for positive contribution. For example, the student's job most certainly possesses characteristics that are relevant to both operant and cognitive approaches. Certain specific behaviors such as promptness in attending class, reading all the way through Chapter 8, and turning in papers on time are appropriate targets for reinforcement.[1] Historically speaking, instructors find that many, if not all, students respond to some very visible and available reinforcers. Grades, comments on term papers, expressions of interest in the student's views — this is the stuff of which reinforcement schedules are made. However, "learning" and "thinking" are not as easily reinforced, specified or propagated. These more global and complex behaviors are believed to be facilitated by a positive attitude or mental state. Could our debaters explain either class of behaviors, simple or complex, using a single model? Yes, and they have in these debates, but only because they have graciously accepted the assignment to pit one model against the other for the specific purpose of highlighting differences between the models. These are reasonable men and women who would most certainly agree that neither model is inherently superior (well, that may be a slight overstatement, but none of them would argue that there is no room for the other model or that all behavior can be explained by a single paradigm.)

To return to our discussion of the practical benefits of understanding both cognitive and operant models, let us take a step backward, before the manager decides how to allocate resources to solve a motivational problem. Before the decisions are made and the budget formulated, a process of inquiry must be undertaken. What theoretical approach will guide the inquiry? Is the motivation problem a result of accidental reinforcement of inappropriate behavior? How many of you know a professor who becomes very angry with a student who has turned in a problem set days late, even though the professor has repeatedly forgotten to collect problem sets on time over the last several weeks? The student gets a message from the professor's absent-mindedness. On the other hand, if the motivational problem seems to be an indirect result of suspicion that there are ethical problems in the executive suite, would we cure this kind of problem the same way we would cure tardiness? No. We would be much more likely to use an operant approach on the first problem and a cognitive approach on the second. Most importantly, would we inquire only into problems and ask only the questions that are prompted by one or the other model, cognitive or operant? No, an inquiry into the problem, otherwise known as research, and a consideration of solutions will be richer and more complete if we retain an open-minded perspective. We hope that the debates have provided you the raw material on which to base inquiry

---

[1] *Editor's note:* This footnote is a test of reinforcement characteristics. If you felt rewarded by reading "Good grief!" in an earlier footnote, reinforcement theorists would predict an increased probability that you would read this one. Did your friends read this one? Maybe nobody did. What would the theorists in both camps say about this?

and the motivation to make use of the best of both cognitive and operant models.

A SHORT REVIEW

As we look back over the four debates and attempt to summarize the compatibilities and incompatibilities of the opposing positions, there are some haunting refrains. To wit:

In Chapter 3 Locke argues in favor of theories and propositions that are logically as well as technologically sound. He pleads that men have minds, and that these minds are necessary elements both in interpreting behavior and in the process of intellectual inquiry. Hamner, his opponent, argues for a particular (operant) logic by presenting a logical argument. While these two debaters may quarrel about the sensibleness, defensibility and completeness of the other's logical process, they share a commitment to logical defense.

In Chapter 4, Fred Luthans argues that an historical analysis of reinforcement patterns (what turns people on) is essential to the use of O.B. Mod. or functional analysis procedures. Pat Smith responds that our job as organizational analysts is to listen, to get to know the world in which the employee lives. Are Fred and Pat all that far apart? Or is the difference between them mostly what they listen to or where they listen — or watch? Certainly they would distinguish between listening and watching on the grounds that self-report techniques may provide different information than behavioral observation; saying is different from doing. But we could well respond to both that both kinds of data enrich our understanding of behavior.

In Chapter 5, the most apparent difference of opinion between Lawler and Cummings centers on the significance of individual differences in understanding the person-job interaction. If we look ahead ten years to a more advanced state of the art, we are likely to find that refined measurement techniques will provide a much more convincing case for individual differences, and incidentally a much better handle on the differences between perceptions and objective reality. If this is the case, then these two debaters are implicitly arguing in favor of scientific advance rather than against each other.

In Chapter 6, Evans and Scott seem to be on very different tracks. I wonder. Marty Evans sees effective leadership as a facilitation process, the process of clearing and clarifying the employee's path to a desired goal, of removing obstacles to goal accomplishment. Bill Scott argues that leadership is arranging reinforcers to reward desired behaviors on the part of subordinates. How far apart are goals and reinforcers? In technical language, miles apart. Conceptually their divergent paths may, in the future, move closer together in pursuit of a common goal.

At a more general level, the four "operant types" (Hamner, Luthans, Cummings and Scott, in case you missed the boat) charge that cognitive models are deficient because we can't see or touch inner states, because they seem to disregard reinforcement history and the impact of the environment. They argue that the operant approach is more effective, by definition, because "it works" and because the implications for applying this approach to changing behavior are more easily specified (see Jablonsky and DeVries, 1972, for examples of management applications). On the other hand, the four "cognitive types" (Locke, Smith, Lawler and Evans) charge that operant models are atheoretical, without theoretical foundation, and do not provide fertile ground for understanding and generalization. They charge that operant models are deficient because one can never know all possible stimuli and responses; that anticipation of the future (a cognition) influences behavior; and that we must acknowledge and encourage individual responsibility. Operant models, they say, require specification of the contingencies of reinforcement and thus limit diversity of effective behavior in organizations.

Can we declare a winner in the operant-cognitive debate? For that matter, can we declare a winner in any of these debates? Not I, never! I declare that important issues have been put on the table for all to consider. I declare that both models have just claims for their continued use and that in many respects each can augment the other. I declare that the purposes to be served by each of these models should be considered in determining their effectiveness (see Karmel, 1978, for a discussion of research purpose). I would further suggest, if not declare, that the cognitive and operant models are, in fact, beginning to merge in such formulations as expectancy, equity and exchange theories. As the state of the discipline becomes more advanced, I would predict intensive examination of the substantive differences and potential for integration.

Steve Kerr has spoken metaphorically about a professor who drops a quarter in the middle of the street but looks for it at the corner because the street lamp is there. Would it be better to continue searching in the darkness, or shall we turn our attention to providing more street lamps? We hope these debates have shed new light on the middle of the street and that the reader will help us look for more quarters.

REFERENCES

Jablonsky, S. F. and DeVries, D. L. Operant conditioning principles extrapolated to the theory of management. *Organizational Behavior and Human Performance*, 7, 1972, 340-358.

Karmel, B. Leadership: A challenge to traditional research methods and assumptions. *Academy of Management Review*, 1978, 3, 475-482.

GLOSSARY OF WORDS AND PHRASES

acognitive:

defining cognitions as irrelevant (the root "a" is a variant of "ab," meaning "away from." Technically, this word should be "abcognitive")

behaviorist:

a psychologist who subscribes to the principles of operant conditioning

behavioristic:

of or pertaining to behaviorism

causal efficacy:

power to bring about effects or results

cognitive:

relating to thoughts or the mind

cognitive theory:

proposition that focuses on thoughts, the mind or internal states as the cause of human behavior

contingencies of reinforcement:

interrelationships of environment, behavior and the consequences of behavior

determinant:

a factor that fixes or conditions an outcome; a cause

environmental determinism:

the devil made me do it; the doctrine which asserts that all of man's beliefs, values, thoughts and actions are necessarily caused by occurrences or conditions outside of himself (in some instances, this term is used interchangeably with "behaviorism")

epiphenomenon:

a secondary phenomenon, not the real thing (in the philosophy of behaviorist psychology, it is asserted that ideas are epiphenomena in that they are incidental by-products of brain activity which cause nothing)

expectancy:

the likelihood that an event will occur; more narrowly, the probability that is attached to event A being followed by event B

explained variance:

technically, the percentage of variation in a dependent variable that can be attributed to one or more independent variables; conversationally, the extent to which one factor accounts for the occurrence of another factor (the presence of clouds explains a great deal of variance in the amount of rainfall)

growth need strength:

a personal or individual attribute relating to the pursuit of intrinsic value in the job (or life); responsibility, challenge and self-actualization are examples

Hegelian dialectic:

an intellectual discourse used to comprehend absolute ideas of which phenomena are partial representations; the pitting of thesis and antithesis in pursuit of synthesis

higher order need strength:

see *growth need strength*

mands:

requirements

mentalistic:

of or pertaining to the mind

model:

a representation of relationships between variables or elements (more formalized than a "list of factors" but not as well developed as a theory)

moderator:

a variable whose presence serves to enhance or strengthen the relationship between two or more other variables (as in, physical size is a moderator in the relationship between sex and ability to lift hay bales)

nexus:

connection; link

operant:

as a noun, the behavior that is instrumental in causing the environment to produce a rewarding or reinforcing effect; as an adjective (operant conditioning), tending to produce effects; in the term "operant model," of or pertaining to instrumental behaviors

paradigm:

pattern; model; map of relationships of elements within a set

parsimony:

the quality of being brief in the statement of ideas or use of resources

pooled variance:

in the specialized use of the term, pooled variance refers to the procedure of averaging over individuals to represent a relationship. Hamner charges that this procedure washes out the very effect (individual uniqueness) that cognitive psychologists claim to be central to their theoretical position

postulate (verb):

claim; propose

(noun):

proposition; hypothesis; assumption

rapprochement:

a state of cordial relations

reification:

ascribing human attributes to inanimate objects

reinforcement theory:

proposition that focuses on the environment and its role in determining human behavior

reinforcer:

consequence of behavior that increases the likelihood of recurrence of the behavior; a stimulus which increases the probability of a response

S_Δ:

events observed by individuals but not perceived to be followed by reinforcers

S_D:

discriminative stimuli; events observed by the individual to be followed by reinforcers

S-O-R:

stimulus-operant-response

tautology:

a statement that is true by virtue of its logical form alone; a logically circular statement